I0081566

NORFOLK's GREATEST
HOME FURNISHERS

The Story of Phillip Levy & Co.

and

The Granby Phonograph

Christopher James Stoessner

6 . 1 . 2 0 1 8

Front Cover Photograph: Phillip Levy & Co. Inc. circa 1919, at the intersection of Main and Church Street, Norfolk, Virginia. Harry C. Mann, Photographer.

Library of Virginia

Granby Phonograph Corporation Factory Illustration Circa 1920

Christopher James Stoessner Private Collection

Copyright. 2018. Christopher James Stoessner

All Rights Reserved. No part of this book shall be reproduced or transmitted in any form by any means, electronic, mechanical, or photographic (to include photocopying, scanning, recording, by any information storage or retrieval system) without prior written permission of the author and/or publisher. Although every precaution has been taken in the preparation of this book, the author extends his apologies but assumes no responsibility for errors and omissions.

All characters, events, and locations in this book are real. Unless otherwise credited or referenced, photographs and documents are property of the author.

If you have any corrections or historical information/data to add, please don't hesitate to contact the author and/or publisher.

James-Gail Co.

www.james-gail.com

christopher@james-gail.com   or   obxfunerals@hotmail.com

ISBN 978-1-7322496-0-8

Library of Congress Control Number 2018905665

l faced type is desired the cost of same will be
ses of advertising on application.

ars'   WANTED—Phonograph salesmen, clean cut,
its   aggressive and experienced live wires. We re-
nu- quire salesmen for Alabama, Florida, Georgia,
At   Mississippi, North Carolina, South Carolina,
ord Tennessee, Virginia and West Virginia. This
king is a real opportunity to grow with a fast grow-
ork   ing manufacturing institution, with a financial
      return dependent entirely upon your ability. Tell
      us your story in detail at once. Confidentially.
hine Granby Phonograph Corporation, Norfolk, Va.
an

get   WANTED—Sole distributor in United States
you for Panhellion brand of Greek and other foreign
ster, language records. Over 200,000 Panhellion rec-

Table of Contents

The keys to our new Granby Street Home have been turned over to us. Already we have a large force at work scouring floors, cleaning windows and getting things in shape. On next Wednesday night we close the doors of our Church street store for good and all. In order to dispose of as much of the remaining stock as possible between now and next Wednesday we have reduced prices even greater than ever before.

Prices Reduced ONE-HALF and More!

Positively not one piece of this stock will be moved. Every article will be sold at some price. If not at retail, then in a lump sum to some speculator. It must go.

It's your chance to furnish or refurnish your home. You can do so now at about one-half what it will cost you later. No matter if it's only a chair you need you can save a half. And if you do not wish to pay cash we will arrange convenient terms.

PHILLIP LEVY & CO.

Norfolk's Greatest Home Furnishers 203-215 Church Street.

The Ledger-Dispatch, Thursday Afternoon, April 21, 1910
Norfolk, Virginia

Prelude

My research on this subject started many years ago. It had a humble and simple beginning. As an amateur antique collector and somebody who appreciates history, I was very intrigued about this *Granby* brand phonograph I had come across at an antiques mall when I was about 18 years old. It said on the tag it was made in Newport News, Virginia - the city in which I was born. To satisfy my curiosity, I began internet research to see if anybody could help tell me about the history of this company. I had questions like...

When were they in business?   Who owned the company?

Doing some quick online research, I learned some basic information about well-known companies like Victor, Edison, Columbia, and others. But, I could find no detailed information about this *Granby* Phonograph. This was turning into a true mystery....

My curiosity then turned into a quest for information and, as anybody who studies history will tell you - the *more* you learn, the more you *want* to know! My trip to the libraries in Newport News and Norfolk turned up a few old ads on microfilm. Company names and logos changed over time which led me to inquire about corporate takeovers. In one year only, a local directory listed the company's officers and owners. Death dates and obituaries gave me survivors and from there I met descendants of the Levy and Coplan family. The story continued to grow and became more and more alive.

What began as a simple quest for information about an antique phonograph turned into a much deeper story about a family, their business operations, and included plot twists and surprises. It drew me in and has become part of me. *A true history enthusiast knows the feeling.* I met numerous kind and helpful individuals, historians, collectors, and persons affiliated with Reliable Stores Corporation of Baltimore (which is an American success story in and of itself.) Even if you are not particularly interested in corporate or business history, I hope you enjoy the details provided in this research. It puts a lot of in perspective, especially in today's business climate of online sales, non-stop television advertising, and more.

Now, after more than fifteen years of research, I am proud to present a complete history of these enterprises with illustrations for reference. It took many hours of research and following creative impulses on possible sources of information, all of which I really enjoyed. It was fun and a challenge at times, like being involved in a movie plot where you don't know what happens next. The Levy family's story is an American success story and has its share of tragedy. It is also a study of economics and corporate history. In this particular case, their furniture stores and phonograph company enjoyed the prosperity of the late teens and early 1920's before being acquired by General Stores Corp. which was merged with Reliable Stores Corp.

Like any history research project, it is never *truly* finished. I am certain there are more pictures, insights, and information that will come available over time. And, if you have something to add, I urge you to *please* contact me. Maybe, there could be future volumes with added photographs and even *more* personal accounts. However, I truly hope you enjoy this work as presented. The story is told in chronological order and is divided into sections. And, yes, it is *very* detailed, but I can take pride in knowing that this part of Virginia and Phonograph history is now well documented. With that said, it can now be assured that history will not forget…

Norfolk's Greatest Home Furnishers
Christopher James Stoessner

Phillip Levy

March 27, 1873 – January 12, 1919

Mr. Levy was the oldest of all the siblings that emigrated from Russia circa 1891. Upon his arrival in America, the siblings made their way to Norfolk where he and his younger brother, Harry, entered the furniture business. He married Esther Levy and they had no children. Phillip died unexpectedly in a train accident in Byron, New York on Jan. 12, 1919 when he was on his way to Grand Rapids, Michigan. At that time, there were 8 stores which grew, expanded, and carried his name for many years after his death under the guidance of his younger brother Harry and, then, the Reliable Stores Corporation after 1924.

Harry Levy

December 15, 1875 – March 7, 1938

A resident of Norfolk, Mr. Levy was a native of Russia, younger brother to Phillip Levy and husband to Celia Reyner of Newport News. After Phillip's untimely death in 1919, he (with Phillip's widow, Esther) inherited and took charge of all of Phillip Levy & Co. furniture stores. Under Harry's direction, the phonograph factory was founded and all companies consolidated under the name American Home Furnishers' Corporation. Harry and Celia had four children; Milton, Isabel, Doris, and Gertrude. I had the distinct pleasure of interviewing Doris back in 2003. She offered clear memories of her father, Harry Levy, and provided insight and a personal touch to this unique story. Her story was special in its own right. She became well known in the Philadelphia area for her interior design skills and was active in charitable organizations. Her recollections are referenced as part of this research.

Part I.   1891 - 1919

The Early Years

Phillip Levy & Co. on Granby Street in Norfolk, Virginia circa 1910

Library of Virginia

The Arrival of Mssrs. Phillip and Harry Levy

In 1891, Phillip Levy and his brother, Harry, left their home in Russia and embarked on their journey to America, ready to start their new life. They were accompanied by their younger sisters, Mary, Rosa, and Sophia. At 18 years old, Phillip was the oldest and Sophia was the youngest, having turned 3 years old on the 11th of June. Within just a few years of their arrival in America, they had made their way south to Norfolk, VA and entered the retail business.

Norfolk is a city in the Hampton Roads region of Virginia that traces its history to the colonial period. The first proposed site for a town was in 1680 in the area then known as Lower Norfolk County. Norfolk was (and is) a strategic shipping area because of access to the Elizabeth River, the Chesapeake Bay, and the Atlantic Ocean. By the year of 1700, the area formerly known as Lower Norfolk County had been divided into Norfolk and Princess Anne County and was home to a few hundred settlers.

As a side note, Princess Anne County no longer exists after its 1963 merger with Virginia Beach, VA. This area, when combined with Chesapeake, Portsmouth, and the Peninsula make up the area commonly known as Hampton Roads or Tidewater.

By the end of the 1700's, the area had grown quite a bit and had a population of well over 5000 settlers and was one of the largest metropolitan areas in Virginia.[1] Throughout the 1800's, Norfolk experienced many ups and downs, including effects from the Civil War, fires, and other growing pains that an urban area encounters. In 1890, Norfolk's population was over 30,000 and home to many immigrants and new businesses that included a variety of industries and retail stores.

After residing on Main Street and using a small room in their basement as a stock room, the Levy brothers purchased Mr. David

---

[1] Carroll Walker, *Norfolk, A Pictorial History* (Virginia Beach, VA: The Donning Co., 1975)

Donovan's furniture business on Church St. and soon expanded. Later in 1909, they were in need of larger quarters and relocated to 209-221 Granby Street, formally opening in May of 1910. This was considered a risky move because Granby Street was in the early stages of development. The location would later be known as the Loew's Theatre and the exterior was very similar to how it appears today as the Roper Center for the Performing Arts.

This impressive store became the *home store* for what became the Phillip Levy chain of furniture stores. The Granby phonograph would also later be named in honor of this sentimental location for the Levy family. When I spoke with Doris Reyner Levy Sostmann, the late daughter of the late Harry Levy, she recalled that ownership in the store was 50/50 but was named for Phillip, being that he was the older of the brothers. When asked if the original intention was to expand, Ms. Sostmann agreed, saying that this expansion would leave a legacy for the family and provide jobs for the large family. She noted that many nephews and family members were appointed managerial and other positions at the various stores.[2]

Phillip Levy & Co. branched out and opened stores in several cities with railroad access including Washington DC, Roanoke, Norfolk, Richmond, Newport News, Franklin, Suffolk, and Savannah, GA. During this period in American history, the railroad was an integral part of everyday life. This was prior to the interstate system that we know today where trucking and automobiles are a major means of transportation. Just as early American population centers developed along waterways, late nineteenth and early twentieth century American towns cropped up along railroads.

In 1916, Phillip and Harry Levy incorporated the American Home Furnishers Corporation with Phillip being the President and Treasurer. The company was established as a separate entity but would later become the parent/umbrella corporation of all of the

---

[2] Sostmann, Doris Reyner Levy. Interview by Christopher J. Stoessner. April 2003.

separate business ventures. Phillip Levy & Co. carried quality furniture and the interior of the stores had an *upscale* appearance. When they first arrived in Norfolk, they advertised dry goods and clothing but by 1901 had started advertising furniture and home furnishings exclusively. Their motto was "better furniture, lower prices, and longer credit." Phillip and Harry Levy were instrumental in the early installment furniture business, a trend in retail that continues to this day. Ms. Sostmann jokingly recalled that "the furniture would almost be worn out before it was paid off under her father's plan." This period in American history was the early age of credit. The full cash price was rarely seen in a furniture store's ad.

Interior View of Phillip Levy & Co.'s Granby Street Store circa 1910

Library of Virginia

We'll Open For Business In Our New Home Monday

After much unavoidable delay, we are now ready for business in our magnificent new Granby street home, which we believe is the finest of its kind in the South. On Monday morning we will throw open our doors to the public. Our "Grand Opening," however, will not take place until a few weeks later.

Complete Line of Furniture, Carpets. Draperies, Mattings, Crockery, Stoves, Office Furniture, Etc., From Lowest to the Highest Grades.

On Account of Our Greater Buying Capacity We are in a Position To Make Prices Even Lower Than it Has Been Our Privilege Before

THE BIG STORE, 209, 211, 213, 215, 217, 219 and 221 GRANBY STREET.

WE WILL CATER TO THE GENERAL PUBLIC-- TRY TO PLEASE ALL

Don't think because we are going into this fine new home that we are going to cater to any exclusive trade. Far from it. It is our purpose to cater to the general public. And, whether it be a bedroom suit at $15 or $150, you will find your wants have been beautifully anticipated here, and because of our better equipment and greater purchasing power we can give you not only better prices but better service.

OUR LIBERAL CREDIT SYSTEM WILL REMAIN UNCHANGED

"Are you going to change your credit system?" This is a question that has been put to us by numerous friends. Emphatically, No! We are going to continue along the same liberal lines that have helped thousands of people to have nicely furnished homes and have made PHILLIP LEVY & CO. famous.

If you wish credit come to us just as you have always done and we will consider it a privilege to accommodate you.

THE BIG STORE, GRANBY STREET. **PHILLIP LEVY & CO.** THE BIG STORE, GRANBY STREET.

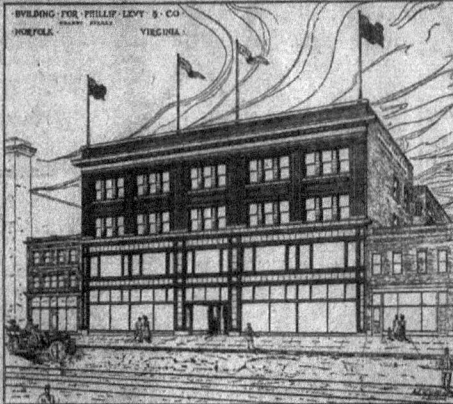

The Ledger-Dispatch, Saturday Afternoon, May 7, 1910

Norfolk, Virginia

8

The Grand Opening of "The Big Store" on Granby Street taken by well-known Norfolk photographer, Mr. Harry C. Mann. The arrows have been inserted in this photograph to show Harry Levy, on the left, and Phillip Levy, on the right. This must have been a very proud moment for the self-made men from Russia.

Library of Virginia

Rugs at Phillip Levy & Co.

Library of Virginia

An Unexpected Tragedy

The Levy brothers were doing well with the expanding chain of furniture stores when the unthinkable happened. In early January of 1919, Phillip had gone on a buying trip to Grand Rapids, Michigan to buy stock for the furniture store when news started to trickle back to Virginia about an accident that occurred on the New York Central Railroad in South Byron, New York. Harry Levy sent a telegram and did not get a response so assuming the worst; he decided to go to New York himself. When Harry left for New York, neither he nor Phillip's wife Esther were certain of his fate on the train.

As of January 14th, details were still unclear back in Newport News and Norfolk, VA. However, that Tuesday morning, the Norfolk store ordered the Newport News store to close for the day in respect to the memory of Phillip Levy. Interestingly enough, the heads of the Newport News store knew nothing of the accident until they read it in The Daily Press that morning. Prior to 11:00 am, nothing had been formally heard from Harry Levy who was said "to be at the scene of the accident, investigating."[3]

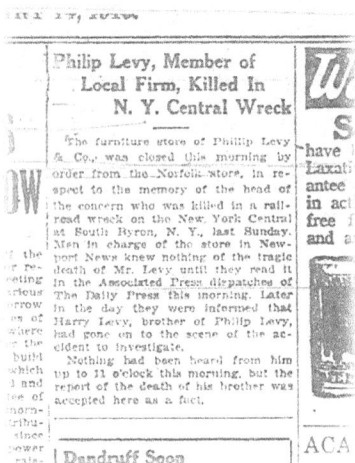

Philip Levy, Member of Local Firm, Killed In N. Y. Central Wreck

Upon Harry's arrival in New York, the full details of the accident could be discerned. While Phillip was on the way to Grand Rapids, he got delayed in New York two days longer than expected. In order to make up for lost time, he took the "Wolverine Limited – Train No. 17." That particular train was a fast train that could travel between New York and Chicago in 18 hours. Unfortunately, the "Southwestern Limited – Train No. 11" (another fast train) collided with the rear and

---

[3] Tuesday, January 14, 1919. The Times-Herald. Newport News, VA. (evening paper)

"telescoped the sleeper attached to the Wolverine Limited" according to phrasing used by newspaper accounts.

The Wolverine had stopped on the track and was waiting for another engine to hitch on to in order to get over a steep grade. The Southwestern Limited was traveling less than 15 minutes behind at a high rate of speed, having left the same station. A flagman was sent out to warn the Southwestern to slow down but it was too late. The engineer only saw the flagman when he was a few car lengths from the Wolverine and hit it going an estimated 50 mph, knocking the Wolverine 250 feet forward. It was said that people up to a mile away could hear the impact. The last sleeping car, called the Canfield, took the brunt of the impact. It crashed into the sleeping car directly in front of it called the Croton Falls which was pushed up at an angle and then crashed back through the Canfield from end to end.[4] Mr. Levy was on the Canfield sleeper car.

From the Collection, Holland Land Office Museum, Batavia, New York

---

[4] https://www.ancestry.se/boards/localities.northam.usa.states.michigan.counties.kent/8812/mb.ashx

22 passengers in that particular car lost their lives and only 1 survived. "Not a sleeping passenger in the car escaped death or serious injury." After the wreck, St. Michael's Church Bell at South Byron was tolled in order to get assistance and nearby funeral parlors were turned into temporary morgues. The wreck was very bad according to newspaper accounts and the "mangled condition" of the bodies slowed the identification process. Ms. Sostmann recalled that when her father arrived on the scene, all of her Uncle Phillip's valuables were missing including identification.

On Thursday, January 16th, a headline told that the body of Phillip Levy had been positively identified by his brother, Harry Levy. He, along with Moe Levy, arrived in Norfolk the evening before, Wednesday, January 15th with his remains. Phillip Levy was only 45 years old at the time of his passing, "in the prime of manhood" according to one newspaper account. Doris Levy Sostmann recalled that this was a very hard time for the family. The brothers were very close and everybody looked up to Phillip being that he was the oldest of all the siblings. The unexpected circumstances of the accident made the situation even more difficult for the grieving family.

Following the accident, the Levy family donated funds to the Norfolk Protestant Hospital (now Sentara Norfolk General Hospital) to build the Phillip Levy Memorial Pavilion which was Virginia's only facility dedicated exclusively to obstetric and maternity care at the time. This was at a time when many births were still occurring at home.[5] As with many living during this time era, Harry and Celia Levy had experience with home births. Their daughter, Doris Reyner Levy, was born at home on November 12, 1912 when they resided at the Shirley Apartments in Norfolk. When filing the official birth certificate, the registrar used the family Bible record as verification.[6]

---

[5] Hailey L. Fehner, et al. Celebrating the Past, Creating the Future. 2013.
[6] Certificate of Birth. Doris Reyner Levy. Nov. 12, 1912

Along with the estimated $96,000.00 that Harry Levy and Phillip's widow Esther donated to the Norfolk Protestant Hospital, there was a life size oil painting of Phillip Levy that hung at the hospital as a tribute and memorial. Phillip Levy and Esther had married on Thursday, April 8, 1897 in Norfolk and they had no children.

The Phillip Levy Memorial Pavilion can be seen on the left in this photograph of the Norfolk Protestant Hospital. *Reprinted with permission by Sentara Healthcare*

In addition to the emotions involved, younger brother Harry now how a budding empire of furniture stores to carry on. After Phillip's death, in February of 1919, Phillip Levy & Co. was incorporated with Harry Levy as President, Phillip's widow Esther being named Vice President, and Harry's wife Celia being named Treasurer. Before this time, the stores had not formally been incorporated with the aforementioned American Home Furnishers Corporation still a different entity at this point in time. It was also during 1919 that the store moved from the location on Granby Street to the intersection of Main and Church Streets in Norfolk.

USE CREDIT

To Start Housekeeping

THE BIG SALE IS OVER

ESTATE OF PHILLIP LEVY HAS BEEN SETTLED

Norfolk's and Newport News' Greatest Furniture Sale is now only a memory. It passed into history when the doors closed Tuesday evening—just as we told you it would. Insofar as this store is concerned, the estate has been settled. The reorganization has been perfected and the business will be continued as Phillip Levy & Co., Incorporated, with

HARRY LEVY, President and General Manager

With Mr. Harry Levy in charge the same policies and progressive business methods will be continued and, to the general public there will be no changes except those which would naturally come to a store of this size from time to time, to make it a still greater Furniture center for Norfolk and the Surrounding Southern States. Our aim today is the same that inspired us back in the little Church Street Store, in our beginning: "To Give Norfolk and Newport News the GREATEST Furniture Store In All The SOUTH," and to make it as easy as possible for every home in this community to enjoy the comforts of a nicely furnished home.

YOUR SMALL ORDER Will Receive the Same Courteous Attention As If You Wanted To Furnish A Hotel	**USE YOUR CREDIT**	**BUY THE THINGS YOU NEED** For your Home NOW. Pay Us A Little Each Pay-Day as **YOU** Get Paid

We Sell You on Credit at Cash Store Prices!

Why can we sell you on credit as cheaply as other stores can sell you for cash? Simply because of our great buying advantage. Instead of saying we'll take a half dozen or dozen of this or that, we say what's the best figure on five or ten carloads—and, when your output reaches the point that you can buy in such quantities, the manufacturer not only grows eager for such orders, but he gets down to "Brass Tacks" and figures prices, never dreamed of by the small buyer. This store is only one of a chain of eight we buy for and others are being contemplated.

Phillip Levy & Company, Inc.

The Big Store   Granby Street, Norfolk

BRANCHES: Richmond, Roanoke, Newport News, Savannah, Suffolk, Petersburg, and 540 Church St., Norfolk
2508 Washington Avenue, Newport News, Va.

The Daily Press, Thursday, March 27, 1919

Newport News, Virginia

Harry Levy, Circa 1923

Christopher James Stoessner Collection

Harry Levy

Harry Levy's late daughter recalls him as being a man of very good taste. He was born on December 15, 1875 and came to America when 15 years old from Russia. On April 3, 1906, he married the former Celia Reyner from Newport News, VA. She was the daughter of leading citizen, Joseph Reyner who sat on the first City Council in Newport News and had a very well-known ship chandling business

15

that carried groceries and many other goods. A reception followed the wedding at the Casino in Newport News. The wedding announcement referred to Harry as a "well known young business man from Norfolk."[7]   Celia's *brother*, Harry Reyner, would later become Mayor or Newport News and became a prominent citizen in his own right. Harry Levy and his wife Celia had four children, Milton, Gertrude, Doris, and Isabel. Ms. Doris Levy Sostmann recalled frequently traveling between Newport News and Norfolk on the ferry, *The Virginia* when she was young.

She remembered her father going on many business trips to oversee the stores and purchase new inventory. There is a family account that he would travel in a private train car. She notes that "he would bring back clothing items for her and her sisters, Isabel, and Gertrude that were stunning and that being a quality that many men unfortunately don't possess this day in age." This is a quality that is important to understand because it explains the style of furniture that the retail stores carried, the manner of display, the advertising, and the quality of the phonographs that would later be produced. These phonographs were designed to match certain home furnishing schemes and would be marketed in that manner. In short, Harry Levy's good taste was apparent in his businesses as well as his personal and family life. The Levy family prospered. They led a fine lifestyle for early 20th century America. Great economic times worked well in their favor. By 1922, Harry was a member of Norfolk's Chamber of Commerce and The Ghent Club.

Harry Levy was interested in aviation. He personally paid the expenses associated with having a parachute jumper come to Richmond in July of 1920 for a Phillip Levy & Co. promotion. At 5:00 pm, Richard Cruickshank of Chicago jumped from the airplane going 80 mph and landed in Sheppard's Field on Monument Avenue

---

[7] March 3, 1906. Levy Wedding Announcement. Daily Press.

in Richmond. The plane had flown to Richmond from Danville, VA and also performed stunts for the crowd.[8]

A publication of the time era, titled Men of the South, noted that Harry "lacked schooling when young but was successful in his business ventures." He was seen as a forward thinking person by his daughter and others in the business community. However, there was one particular instance where Harry Levy's creativity in salesmanship did not prove to be such a great idea. In January of 1914, Phillip Levy & Co. made an attempt to collect on money owed by Ms. Gertrude Davis of Norfolk and filed a civil lawsuit to obtain the funds. The court found the evidence and claim to be in favor of Phillip and Harry's furniture store, however, the court ruled in favor in Ms. Davis. *Why?*

It turned out that Ms. Davis operated a house of prostitution in Norfolk. Not only did Harry Levy suggest furnishings for the business but being the progressive business man that he was, he further suggested that Ms. Davis enlarge her business to meet the demands of the sailors aboard the battleships for when they returned to port in Norfolk. He informed her that this would increase her profits. In that day in age, the court frowned on Harry Levy's knowledge and participation in the business transaction, even though he was not *directly* involved with Ms. Davis or her business. The court officially announced that all were equally guilty in an immoral transaction and would not lend its support to the collections process.[9] This proves to be an interesting side story that does not tarnish Harry Levy's legacy but rather proves his (maybe questionable) creativity in a very early and moral period in Hampton Roads history.

When it came to advertising, the marketing that was utilized for the retail operations was very innovative. Phillip Levy & Co. had a very aggressive newspaper marketing campaign that included many sales, promotions, and other unique styles of advertising. One of these

---

[8] July 26, 1920. Richmond Times Dispatch. Ad.
[9] Phillip Levy & Co. vs. Davis. Supreme Court of Appeals of VA. Jan. 15, 1914.

unique ads was in the form of a letter. These "letter style ads" would explain everything from wages, lumber prices and how they affected furniture prices, and also included simple "thank you" style letters. All ads were signed, *"Harry Levy, President."* This was unique retail marketing. Think of the time period…. This was 1920, before the days of TV commercials and email marketing. Harry Levy believed in marketing and newspaper advertising. For example, in 1923, American Home Furnishers Corporation allocated $250,000.00 for newspaper advertising among all the stores.[10]

Although Phillip Levy & Co. was based in Norfolk, the Richmond branch maintained a constant presence in the Richmond Times Dispatch.

---

[10] American Home Furnishers Corporation. A Story in Pictures.

Harry Coplan Makes a Proposal

In addition to keeping up with the latest home furnishing trends, Harry Levy was intrigued by another fast growing segment of American business – the phonograph. He was already very familiar with the product from his many years in the retail business. But, in 1919, there was a loyal employee and manager of Phillip Levy & Co. on Washington Ave. in Newport News that had been studying the concept for the better part of four years. His name was Harry Coplan and his proposal was that, instead of purchasing phonographs *wholesale* from Columbia Phonograph Co. or Aeolian, as they had been, why not manufacture the phonograph themselves, in their own factory, in *Newport News, VA*?

Harry Coplan was born April 21, 1891 in Pinsk, Russia and, like the Levy family, had immigrated to America to start his new life. Upon his arrival in America, he met and married the former Fannie Markel from Richmond, VA and had two children, Asher and Marvin. Harry had settled in Newport News by this point in time and was moving up the ranks in the home furnishings business. He was only 27 years old prior to April of 1919 when these developments were taking place.

Mr. Coplan organized his ambitious ideas and made a formal proposal to Phillip Levy & Co. His proposal included a plan to purchase a large piece of property, erect a factory, and manufacture their own brand of phonograph for distribution in the Phillip Levy network of stores. This project and concept was large in scope. But, possibly to Mr. Coplan's surprise, he got his answer – yes. He was instructed to go forth and purchase a site. One could only imagine the feeling that Mr. Coplan had when he was told to go forward with this idea. Furthermore, one could only imagine the amount of sales revenue and capital that Phillip Levy & Co. had at their disposal to simply say "yes." Mr. Coplan was responsible for the establishment and growth of the retail store in Newport News and would now retire and devote himself fully to the phonograph factory. A banquet was held at the Hotel Warwick in Newport News, VA and where the formal announcement was made.[11] The Phillip Levy & Co. store on Washington Ave. was left in the capable hands of John J. Talman and Percy Trilnick.

Left: Percy Trilnick   Right: Unidentified   Circa 1921

Photograph Courtesy of Sarah Siegler

---

[11] Presto, page 25, May 29, 1920 *and* Presto, page 26, April 24, 1920

Like Norfolk, Newport News has a long and prominent history going back to the founding of the United States. It occupies a peninsula in the Hampton Roads region of southeastern VA that it shares with the current City of Hampton, York County, James City County, and the City of Williamsburg. It is home to the Newport News Shipbuilding and Dry Dock Co. which was started in 1886 by Collis P. Huntington. Prior to that, in 1880, the Chesapeake and Ohio railroad had been extended to the area and much growth occurred as a result. The city was incorporated in 1896 and later consolidated with the former Warwick County in 1958, creating the present day city limits. According to a 1921 publication entitled, *Newport News, Virginia, The Harbor of a Thousand Ships*, the area claimed, "pure water, excellent schools, nine banks with deposits exceeding 14 million dollars, over 35,000 inhabitants," and also, "important terminal facilities with seven miles of Harbor frontage, twenty four hour freight service to New York, and twelve hour freight service to Baltimore and Washington."

Harry Coplan's connection to the area and Harry Levy's *Reyner* family connections (through his wife, Celia) made Newport News an attractive option for a phonograph factory – in addition to its strategic location and close proximity to Norfolk.

Why Manufacture *Phonographs* ?

In order to fully understand the appeal to Harry Levy of this grand scheme of Harry Coplan's to manufacture phonographs, one must know a little background on the economic conditions and the phonograph business during this period. This was the period right after World War I which had just come to a conclusion in November of 1918. Woodrow Wilson was President and there were only 48 states. You could buy two boxes of cereal for 25 cents and a dozen eggs cost around 55 cents. Going out to a movie could cost as high as 30 cents for an evening showing. Important to *this* story is the fact that home furnishings and household goods were surging in sales during this post war period. Included in this surge in sales was the

21

phonograph, not the small and *primitive* cylinder playing phonograph that Thomas Edison invented but *cabinet models* that came in a variety of shapes and sizes that now dominated the marketplace. By this time, the Victor Talking Machine Company of Camden, New Jersey, the Columbia Graphophone Company of Bridgeport, Connecticut, and other national companies such as Brunswick and Edison dominated the trade. Victor "Victrolas" and Columbia "Grafonolas" were a household name and very well-known due to their national advertising campaigns and network of wholesalers and retailers. They had been in business since the turn of the century and had a plethora of patents that protected their unique features. Patents covered every detail of the machine including, in some instances, the size and shape of the tone arm, the style of the doors that opened in front of the internal horn (on the cabinet models), and other characteristics. An example that immediately comes to mind is the Columbia Grafonola's unique shutter style doors that controlled volume on their cabinets. Each company had a feature that made their product unique.

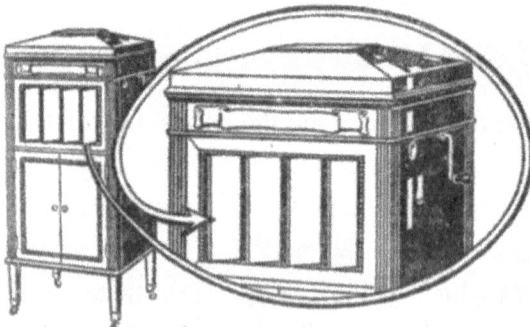

Look for the
TONE LEAVES

Exclusive Columbia Features

These *exclusive* Tone Leaves identify every genuine Columbia Grafonola. You know, when you see them, that the phonograph before you has all the important *exclusive* features.

These *exclusive* Tone Leaves will give you complete and accurate control over tone volume without sacrificing tone

The Daily Press, November 11, 1920, Newport News, Virginia

Truthfully, at this point in time, phonograph technology had not changed *that much* for the past 10 to 15 years. However, just as it happens to this day, the marketplace desired something new and exciting. The concept and science of sound reproduction had not changed, however, the cabinet – the piece of furniture the mechanism is housed in, certainly *could* change. The phonograph was starting to become valued for its place in the home as a piece of furniture, a focal point, more than just a novelty or entertainment device. Columbia, Victor, and others had started this trend a few years before but it was catching on at a fast pace by this point in history, attracting other companies to get into the industry.

In every region across America, local department stores, music stores, and furniture stores were happy to meet the public's demand and, not necessarily with one of the big prominent phonographs, but with their own "phono-brand." Some stores would buy a complete phonograph from a third party and simply put their own name on it. There are numerous machines in existence with the name of a small family owned furniture store under the lid and no other nameplates or

Phonograph Cabinets

that are the product of mas-
ter-craftsmen—skilled in fine
cabinet work for twenty-five
years. Only five-ply selected
woods are used — Genuine
Mahogany—Quartered Oak
—American Walnut. The
finish is high grade and per-
manent. Eight different
styles at reasonable prices.
A word from you will
bring full information immediately.

46 in. high
19½ in. wide
21½ in. deep

The Celina Specialty Company
Celina, Ohio

serial numbers. Other stores would take it one step further. They would go to Grand Rapids, Michigan and buy the furniture/cabinet portion and then purchase the mechanism parts such as the motor, hardware, and other components wholesale and assemble it themselves in a small regional factory. It is important to note, not all projects were small in scope, national stores like Sears offered its own brand of phonograph called the Silvertone and Montgomery Ward offered its own Cecilian "Melophonic" phonograph.

23

Grand Rapids was a large center for furniture production in the United States at this point in time. The area had semi-annual furniture conventions geared towards retailers and other prospects. Many downtown buildings were solely used for phonograph exhibits by the end of the teens. Furniture manufacturers were catering to a growing trend. People wanted phonographs and the emphasis was on *cabinetry.* By October 6, 1920, Grand Rapids was being overwhelmed with orders for phonograph cabinets and the manufacture had seriously cut into the production of traditional furniture. Furniture manufacturers were either:

> **1.** turning over their facilities and production energy to 100% phonograph making,
>
> **2.** *partly* doing this, or
>
> **3.** renting out warehouse and other production space to the companies that *were* doing it.

For example, well known piano makers, The Aeolian Co. rented the 4 upper floors of the Nelson-Matter warehouse at the foot of the Lyon Street Bridge in Grand Rapids to use as a phonograph assembling plant. The well-known Widdicomb Furniture Company had also gotten into the phonograph business by 1919. They were established in 1873 and one account from the time era noted them as the largest bedroom manufacturer in the world. Even long established businesses knew that there was too much income potential in talking machine cabinet production to stay on the sideline.

Although many stores and wholesalers were getting in on the action, retail furniture stores had slightly more to benefit. An interesting article appeared in Talking Machine World, a publication geared towards the phonograph trade, about the benefits to the furniture store of offering fine phonographs. The article claimed that "richness in design and finish of talking machines arouses desires for home furnishings." The theory was simply that in 1919 – 1920, if somebody were to buy a fancy phonograph and place it in a home that wasn't properly furnished; the phonograph would look "glaringly out of place." Or… the rest of the furniture would look out of place. It goes without saying that this concept didn't *always* apply. Some consumers would select phonographs that would fit in their current furnishing scheme and some consumers just wanted a nice phonograph and were not worried about the rest of the room. However, the article makes an interesting point. The potential was there for more sales and this gave furniture stores an opportunity to establish trusting and lasting relationships with the customer. This process would create a new desire for matching furniture schemes and period furniture was coming into vogue at this time. Enter Phillip Levy & Co. and Harry Levy's good taste. He would take this concept and run with it.

The *properly* furnished Dining Room can be seen in this Phillip Levy & Co. window display shown in a 1923 publication published by American Home Furnishers Corp.

Christopher James Stoessner Collection

Characteristics of an "Off Brand" Phonograph

One doesn't have to be a phonograph collector or historian to need to be familiar with the term, "off brand phonograph." This umbrella term covers a wide category of machines and novelty phonographs *not* manufactured by the large national companies mentioned in the previous section. It is true that many of the "off brand" companies were small. But, some companies grew, prospered, and became a thorn in the side of the companies like Victor, Columbia, and Edison – to name a few. The Vitanola Talking Machine Co. of Wabash Ave. in Chicago is an example. They were quite successful and well known in their day. Other companies were more of a "one gimmick" kind of company with a catchy name or logo.

See the New

Crystola

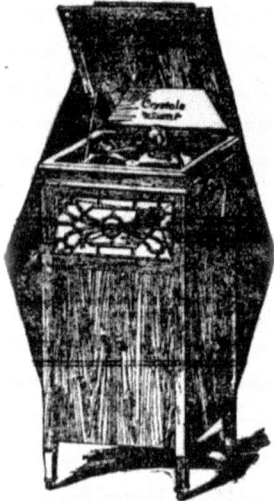

The Phonograph With the Wonderful Mirror Plate **Glass Tone Amplifier**

Not like any other phonograph you ever heard. Wonderfully superior and more human in its reproduction of all

A notable phonograph currently in my own private collection was made by the Crystola Company of Cincinnati, Ohio. The internal horn was made out of mirrored glass and the cabinet featured glass door knobs on the record storage compartment. But, an account of the time era noted that the glass would sometimes get broken in transit to the final retail destination. However, the gimmick was the marvelous sound reproduction through the glass horn… *definitely unique.*

There are also varying degrees of manufacture with these smaller companies. *As previously mentioned*, some companies completely manufactured their product from scratch and some bought the parts from other companies and merely assembled the final product.

Another important feature of most, if not all, of the off brand phonographs from this era is the Universal Tone Arm. This was a key feature in the "appeal" of the phonograph. The universal tone arm could play both types of 78 rpm records that were currently on the market, Lateral Cut and Vertical Cut records. In vertical cut records, the sound vibrations were stored in the bottom of the record groove. When the needle traveled up and down in the grooves, it would reproduce the sound waves and amplify them acoustically through the internal horn. In lateral cut records, a similar process existed but this time, sounds vibrations were stored in the side of the grooves.[12] The universal tone arm could pivot and play both of these styles of records. Any machine that featured this tone arm proudly displayed "plays all records" in their ads. Many of the big name companies were not interested in this style of tone arm. They had too much invested in *their* own recording technique and only wanted the consumer to buy *their* records. Their machines would play either lateral **or** vertical, whereas the new up and coming "off brand" phonographs with the universal tone arm would play *both*.

HERE IT IS
The
FLETCHER UNIVERSAL
TONE ARM and REPRODUCER
Gives Proper Playing Weights for all Records.   No Adjustment Screws or Springs.
SAMPLES $8.00   Specify 8½" or 9½" arm
FLETCHER-WICKES CO., 6 East Lake Street, Chicago, Illinois
THE GEORGE McLAGAN FURNITURE CO., STRATFORD, ONTARIO, EXCLUSIVE CANADIAN AGENTS

[12]Taylor, Todd. *Vinyl Audities.*

Enter The Leviola

Following Phillip's untimely death, it was now Harry Levy's job to observe and act on these market trends and Mr. Coplan made a good case. The American Cabinet Manufacturing Corporation was incorporated on April 16, 1919 in Virginia with Harry Levy as President, Charles F. Pitt as Vice President, and Harry Coplan as Secretary and Treasurer. Both Mr. Pitt and Mr. Coplan resided in Newport News. Mr. Pitt had operated a cabinet making company on 30th Street for many years. Although officially incorporated to "manufacture furniture specialties and fixtures of all kinds," the factory had one thing in mind, *the Leviola*. Later that same year, on September 6, 1919, the Leviola Talking Machine Sales Corporation was incorporated. Harry Levy was also President of this enterprise, with F. Percy Loth as First Vice President, William A. Godwin as Second Vice President, and Tazewell Taylor as Secretary. All gentlemen were from Norfolk with the exception of Mr. Loth who was from Waynesboro and was associated with the well-known W. J. Loth Stove Co. The Leviola corporation was the business/selling enterprise and American Cabinet was the manufacturing division. They were separate entities, *for now*.

The Leviola was a tall upright phonograph made of genuine mahogany and in period design. As previously mentioned, period furniture was coming into popularity and furniture stores had a lot to benefit by selling this style of phonograph. The name was derived from the Levy name and the addition of the "ola" suffix seen on many cabinet phonographs following the example of the Victrola. The Leviola would play any disc on the market, "perfectly and clearly." The tone and volume of the music was "marvelous" which eliminated the scratching sound heard on other makes of machines. It stood 48 and ½ inches tall and was 27 ½ inches deep. It had a twelve inch turntable, needle cups, and a compartment for albums that were furnished with the machine designed to hold 10 and 12 inch 78 rpm records. Brass trimmings and casters (small wheels) came standard.

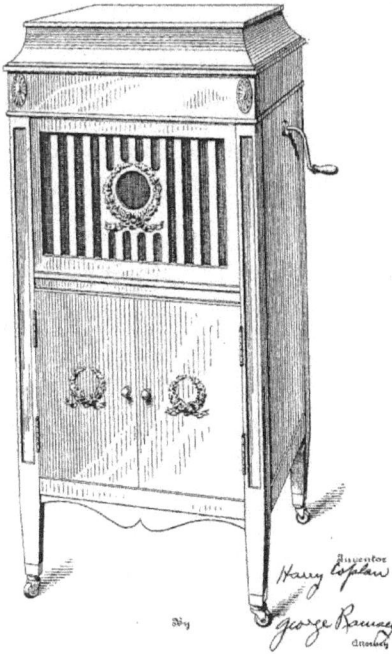

Applying the finish to the Leviola was quite a detailed process. Varnish was applied on the second floor of the original factory building after staining and filling had occurred. Leviolas were placed on a revolving table and the varnish was applied with an air gun. The phonograph cabinet was then taken to a room with a temperature of over 100 degrees, where it remained for over 24 hours. The machines were then given to the "rubbers" who applied their products and left a "perfectly glazed varnished surface."

29

As the 1919 Christmas retail season approached, there was no sign of the Leviola until November 16th. On this date, Phillip Levy & Co. placed a very large ad in Newport News' Daily Press declaring that on Monday, 200 Leviola Phonographs would be sold on a "first come, first served basis." This large ad overshadowed every other ad in the paper and made the introduction of the Leviola appear like *quite an event*. The Leviolas were sold at a discounted price of $175.00. The ad stated that they would return to their regular retail price of $225.00 once the phonographs were sold and this promotion was over. The ad also stated that this was "Phillip Levy & Co.'s way of properly introducing the Leviola to the people of Newport News." A similar advertising campaign was seen in The Virginian-Pilot for the Norfolk branch of Phillip Levy & Co.

Following the stores' proclamation of this being "positively the most striking, startling, and astonishing phonograph announcement ever made to the people of Newport News," an intense marketing campaign ensued through the local newspapers in the respective store's territory. This phonograph was marketed to all walks of life including bankers, merchants, and the laboring man. Following the initial introduction, another ad noted that the Leviola could be purchased for $5.00 down with the remaining balance being paid in "small payments to suit your convenience." Furthermore, the Leviola could be returned in 10 days for a full refund if the customer was not satisfied. The phonograph was guaranteed for 12 months and Phillip Levy & Co. was quick to convey how much they believed in their product. When referring to the guarantee, they pointed out that the President and officers of the company behind the offer were "well known in the community." They also noted that the guarantee was backed by a "concern capitalized at 2.5 million dollars." It is interesting to observe the transparency and pride in Phillip Levy & Co.'s advertising. Unlike some businesses who are very private and protective of their net worth and income, they were proud of their business and didn't mind stating the facts in order to make their point. The initial sale and introduction sold 43 of the 200 machines. A later ad reminded potential buyers that after the remaining 157 are sold, the price would return to the regular retail price of $225.00.[13]

By the time December came around, the Leviola occupied a regular and prominent place in all advertising by Phillip Levy & Co. It usually had a complete "block" devoted to it in order to make it stand out. Interestingly, the Leviola was marketed as a "third party" piece of merchandise in some ads. Customers were urged to look for the trademark and that none were genuine unless the trademark was present. At this point in time, you had a choice of phonographs if you walked into one of the Phillip Levy stores. You could purchase a Columbia Grafonola, Aeolian-Vocalion Phonograph, or the Leviola.

The Daily Press, Christmas Eve, December 24, 1919

Newport News, Virginia

---

[13]November 21, 1919. Daily Press. Ad.

As Christmas drew closer, ads could be seen almost every day for Phillip Levy & Co. with the Leviola emphasized. Completely separate ads were also being *simultaneously* run for the Leviola. This campaign urged buyers to hurry in to get "the wonder machine of the phonograph age" in time for Christmas. The customer could still return it in 10 days if not completely satisfied. Advertising for the Leviola slowed down after Christmas of 1919. The store had certainly met the demand and had the marketing campaign to go with it!

Harry Levy *must* have been pleased with Harry Coplan's proposal and ultimate results. After some experimentation, Leviola production started back on June 10, 1919 and Mr. Levy originally budgeted for a financial loss the first year. This was not the case. By December of 1919, over 4000 Leviolas had been produced and sent out to the Phillip Levy chain of stores including Savannah and Baltimore. The impressive Leviola sales figures of 1919's Christmas season brought on a major development. On February 2, 1920, the Board of Directors met in Norfolk and decided to file an amendment to the charter of the Leviola Talking Machine Sales Corporation changing the name to Granby Phonograph Corporation. No officers or stock amounts changed. Granby Phonograph Corporation of Norfolk also shows up in the Newport News City Directory for the first time in 1920. It was listed at the corner of 26th Street and Virginia Ave. (now Warwick Blvd.). The corporation was named after the famed Granby Street in Norfolk, site of the prominent home store of Phillip Levy and Company, *although* it have moved to the corner of Main and Church Street by this time.

There is also a separate listing for American Cabinet Manufacturing Corporation at the same site as Granby Phonograph Corporation in the Newport News City Directory. These companies were being operated as separate business structures - the sales company, and the manufacturing division. The newly named Granby Corporation had much bigger plans than the Leviola Corporation, hence the name change. The Leviola was a regional phonograph that was meant to be sold through the Phillip Levy & Co. stores and was never advertised in national publications like Talking Machine World and other trade journals. However, Granby Phonograph Corporation was going *national*.

Exit **the Leviola**

September 1, 1920 brought another big sale of talking machines, similar in scope to the initial introduction. Except, these phonographs were not called by name and there was no talk of trademarks. There are four phonographs pictured, some of which are the illustrations seen previously in 1919 then referred to as Leviolas. This was a liquidation sale! It appears that during this transitionary period of the company name change, an attempt was made to clear out Leviolas.

Evidence shows that up to *four* Leviola models were produced and they were offered at retail prices of $135, $150, $160, and $185.00. This liquidation sale showed the prices lowered to $97.50 for the $135 and $150 models. The models previously listed at $160 and $185 were offered at the discounted price of $118.75. They were advertised as "standard make and recognized quality." Phillip Levy & Co. stressed the point that the low prices did not mean these phonographs were substandard quality. They were as perfect as they day they left the factory and had "been used in various stores for demonstration." They were still guaranteed for one year and included 10 records, free of charge. If a down payment was made, the customer could pay $1.50 per week until the balance was paid off. It was unclear of how many Leviolas were made but a serial number of 18,927 exists in my private collection. The Leviola occupies an important place in this story, *although very short lived.*

AMERICAN CABINET MANUFACTURING CORPORATION

MANUFACTURERS OF

HIGH CLASS PERIOD TALKING MACHINES

MAIN UNIT OF PLANT, SHOWING VIRGINIA AVENUE SIDE

Manufacturing a High-Grade Product for Nation-Wide Distribution

The purpose of the builders of this plant is to place within the reach of every family at a minimum cost the highest-grade Talking Machines it is possible to make. Perfection, or as near perfection as human ingenuity can attain, is our object, and in the making of the Talking Machines in this plant QUALITY shall be the keynote, ever bearing in mind that the talking machine that will ultimately be most popular with the music-loving people of America will be the talking machine that combines the largest number of tonal qualities, reproducing perfectly the original renditions, whether vocal or instrumental, and a substantial cabinet made from the best woods, that will be a handsome addition to the fittings for any home, however finely furnished.

JOBBERS OF TALKING MACHINE RECORDS AND NEEDLES

THE MOST MODERN PLANT OF ITS KIND IN THE ENTIRE SOUTH

26th to 27th Streets on Virginia Avenue and C. & O. Railroad, Newport News, Virginia.

The Daily Press, May 2, 1920, Newport News, Virginia

Part II.   1920

The Rise of the American Home Furnishers Corporation

The corporation's central warehouse in Norfolk

Christopher James Stoessner Collection

Reorganization & Consolidation

1920 was proving to be a pivotal year in the story of Harry Levy's enterprises. It had only been one year since his brother Phillip's death. And, his business associate Harry Coplan's phonograph venture was proving to be an overnight success. Now, faced with a chain of furniture stores *and* a factory, a little reorganization was in order. On July 27, 1920, a merger was filed in the State of Virginia bringing three of the corporations under one name; American Home Furnishers Corporation. Keep in mind, this corporation was originally incorporated on April 27, 1916. However, this merger brought in Phillip Levy & Co. and the American Cabinet Manufacturing Corporation. Going forward, these three companies would not be separate entities but would be operated in the manner that many businesses operate today; a corporate name with different fictitious or "trade names" that would be filed locally and used as "divisions." Today, many well-known automobile names, restaurants, and retail stores are operated as a brand or trade name with a completely different corporation name – perfectly legal and common in the business world.

However, Granby Phonograph Corporation would remain separate from the American Home Furnishers Corporation umbrella. It would remain a wholly owned subsidiary. In *simple language*, Granby was kept a separate entity but owned by the same stockholders that owned the stock in American Home Furnishers Corporation. There were 60,000 shares of stock issued of which 15,000 where preferred stock, 15,000 class A common stock, and 30,000 shares of class B common stock. Harry Levy owned the 15,000 shares of preferred stock as of the filing of this merger agreement. The officers were Harry Levy – President/Treasurer, Esther Levy – Vice President, William. A. Godwin – Second Vice President, Hugo. H. Shumaker – Secretary, and Maxwell L. Coplan, (Harry Coplan's brother) Assistant Secretary. All individuals resided in Norfolk, VA.

This should be noted as an important part of business history. This merger and consolidation proved to be a model that businesses follow to this day. All this was occurring in the Hampton Roads region of Virginia but would have a national effect. With the Leviola Corporation now renamed and the merger behind him, Harry Levy was ready to take this operation to the next level – national phonograph production and distribution.

YOUR CREDIT IS GOOD HERE

PHILLIP LEVY & C⁰.

DIV.

AMERICAN HOME FURNISHERS' CORP.
2508 WASHINGTON AVENUE
NEWPORT NEWS, VA.

Other Connections:
Norfolk, Va.
Richmond, Va.
Roanoke, Va.
Franklin, Va.

Other Connections:
Baltimore, Md.
Savannah, Ga.
Suffolk, Va.

Advertisements after this point in time featured the American Home Furnishers' Corporation name underneath (or close to) the furniture store trade name.

The Daily Press, Wednesday, September 1, 1920

Newport News, Virginia

37

The Granby Phonograph Emerges in Newport News, Virginia

After 10 days of heavy advertising in early September of 1920 in an effort to sell off Leviolas and models used for demonstration, there was a month lull in phonograph advertising for Phillip Levy & Co. However, ads for traditional furniture and stoves were still frequent. A large ad devoted completely to a Granby Phonograph appeared in the Daily Press on October 27, 1920 and was worded like something not previously advertised. The caption reads, "This phonograph, that you see in our window, you may have in your home on the payment of $5.00." The ad goes on to reassure the public that their wait for a phonograph was well worth it and "the Granby was worth waiting for." The "phonograph of phonographs" was offered for $5.00 down and $2.00 a week until paid off. This became the standard promotion of 1920 from the masters of the installment business – Phillip Levy & Co. The Granby was described as "way ahead in tone, beauty of design and perfection of motor" and being built of the "sum total of phonograph experience behind it." *This is a reference to the success of the Leviola.*

Other information also alluded to the fact that the Leviola had provided insight into the phonograph market and proved valuable in the formation of Granby Phonograph Corporation. An article that appeared in the August 15, 1920 edition of Talking Machine World read, "the talking machine (manufactured by American Home Furnishers Corporation for sale in its many warerooms in Norfolk and vicinity) grew rapidly in popularity and the heavy demand for it led to the formation of Granby Phonograph Corporation and the sale of Granby Phonographs throughout the country."

The local advertising that ensued during 1920 featured three phonographs in Mahogany, Oak, or Burled Walnut finishes. The

Model A carried a price of $185.00, the Model B was $135.00 and the Model C was $115.00. Of all three models, the Model B was emphasized and most advertising featured it only. Separate Granby Phonograph ads were run apart from Phillip Levy & Co., who was the only Granby distributor in Newport News and Norfolk. The ads featured specials on records, usually "Mamie Smith and her Jazz Hounds." Of particular interest is an ad that appeared in the Daily Press on December 10, 1920 for a "lot of Granby phonographs at ½ price." This was run by Newport News Phonograph Repair and Supply Co. One can only imagine how they got their hands on this new phonograph for such a bargain. *Maybe they had flaws or were rejects from the factory…* One thing is certain, though; they were told not to use the Granby name in an ad again. The next ad that ran on December 19th read, "lot of *High Grade* phonographs" instead of the Granby name.

The Granby Phonograph was advertised as a "third party" machine, meaning Phillip Levy & Co. rarely mentioned the fact that they were very closely associated with the production of it during this early period. *Later* ads mention a sense of local pride in the purchasing of the phonograph. The line "built right here in Newport News" is featured in some ads and goes on to say that the Granby "is one of the finest built and finest looking phonographs turned out by any factory." One unique ad goes right for the *local pride effect* and states that the Granby "is built to order right here in Newport News…. And you may well feel proud of it." Records and phonograph needles were usually given away free but the price of the phonograph could not be reduced because they were "of standard make strictly guaranteed." All ads from 1920 and beyond featured the regular terms of $5.00 down and $2.00 weekly payments. One particular ad stated that Phillip Levy & Co. wanted to put a Granby Phonograph in every home in Newport News. Buying a phonograph was compared to purchasing smoking tobacco according to the ads. However, this particular "modest outlay" would get the customer a "perfect musical instrument" and "a decided ornamentation for the home."

The Leviola and Granby Connection

During this transitionary period of time when the company changed names, it is interesting to note, although the phonographs are referred to as Granbys, the illustrations seen in the newspaper ads look *a lot like* the illustrations previously referred to as Leviolas. There are a few different theories that could be introduced:

1. Did the remaining Leviolas get a new logo and begin being called Granby Phonographs? This would mean that there are Granby phonographs that were not featured in the national product line and would have only been advertised locally around Newport News and Norfolk until sold out.

2. Did the Daily Press not receive the right artwork/copy and were they using recycled images from previous ads? *Possible...* but highly unlikely. Phillip Levy & Co. did specific advertising saying "$5.00 puts *this* Granby Phonograph in your home." Model designation and information is given, accompanied by the coordinating illustrations. It is not likely that a reputable store would allow an extensive advertising campaign to occur without the correct illustrations.

MODEL A—PRICE, $185.00
A distinguished design with a cabinet most beautifully finished. Your choice of mahogany, oak or buried walnut.

After doing some modern day research (and some antique phonograph hunting...), it now appears to that theory **number one** proves to be correct. A Granby phonograph has been located that is almost identical in design to a Leviola. It has a different grill and different logo only. Apparently, it is quite likely remaining Leviola stock got re-branded and advertised as Granby Phonographs until the stock was sold out.

The Granby Phonograph Factory

Christopher James Stoessner Collection

Harry Coplan's dream and concept was now a reality. Harry Levy and American Home Furnishers Corporation had established a full-fledged phonograph factory in downtown Newport News, VA. What began as a modest building producing Leviolas, this impressive building now occupied the *entire* block between 26th and 27th streets intersecting with Virginia Ave (now Warwick Blvd.) Although from Norfolk, Harry Levy's late daughter, Doris Levy Reyner Sostmann, recalled that the site was chosen because of its close proximity to the railroad and because of her mother's family connections in Newport News. She believed the property originally belonged to her grandfather, Joseph Reyner. Remember, his daughter, the former Celia Reyner had married Harry Levy. Celia's brother, Harry Reyner who sat on City Council for 12 years went on to become Mayor of Newport News. He is credited with coming up with the City Farm concept according to Ms. Sostmann. She remembers her Uncle commenting on how it made more sense to have inmates performing practical duties instead of sitting in a jail or prison. He went on to become Vice President of Granby in 1923.

Although the Reyner connection was strong, it was Harry Coplan who had secured and purchased the site with Harry Levy's blessing according trade journal accounts. It fronted the Chesapeake and Ohio Railroad and represented an initial investment of $250,000.00 and when the machinery was taken into account, was closer to $350,000.00. When hardware, other equipment, lumber, and finished Granbys ready for delivery, the total value of the operation in 1920 was $750,000.00. It was constructed of brick, concrete, and was fireproof throughout.

Everything did not go smoothly in the beginning. When the building was first built back in 1919, it was without "sewerage" and the roads had not been paved in this section of Newport News. After butting heads with city officials, the American Home Furnishers Corp. noted that they would "take the matter into their own hands" for sewer facilities instead of waiting on the City.

In September of 1919, attorney Phillip W. Murray presented his request at City Council and requested paving of nearby roads including Virginia Ave. and 26th St. He noted that the tax revenue from the factory would help offset paving costs. Several council members spoke in favor and in opposition of the new concrete roads. The newspaper account referred to the factions as "concretists and anti-concretists." Ultimately, the "concretists" won out and the road to the Boat Harbor and other areas in question were allowed to be paved with 6" concrete at a cost of $3.18 per yard.

On August 3rd, 1920, after a luncheon in Newport News, Harry Levy led a tour of over 100 Rotarians through the factory.[14] They were very impressed with what they saw! An article in the August 15, 1920 issue of Talking Machine World offers a plethora of information about the factory.

---

[14] "Rotarians Guests of Granby Co." TMW. 8-3-1920. Page 208.

When the building was first constructed, 100 Leviolas could be built per day but this larger operation could produce 225 Granby phonographs per day in the factory of "the most approved fireproof construction." The Granby Corporation kept growth in mind because the foundation of the building was built so that 2 to 3 stories could easily be added. Granby also owned "considerable adjoining land where outward growth" was possible. The Pabst Building and Royal Warehouse in Newport News were leased as they struggled to meet demand in the coming years.

When lumber arrived via the railroad, a private track carried it to the "$40,000 Sturtevant high humidity dry kilns close by." Each machine in the factory was equipped with its own motor, of which electricity powered. The woodworking equipment was "the most modern known in the trade." According to accounts from the time era, Granby spared no expense. Efficiency was stressed, from one end of the factory where the kilns were located all the way to the other end where the final phonograph was boxed and shipped. Each process involved in the manufacturing process was done in a manner that involved "the least amount of motion." The "proper machine for the proper purpose" was used by Granby.

A rare interior view of the "mill room" at the factory

Christopher James Stoessner Collection

Granby Phonographs were built with 7/8 "five ply" veneer panels of which 4 coats of varnish were given. The phonographs could be shipped by boat "to every port on both the Atlantic and Pacific coast." The factory's location on the railroad and close proximity to the harbor was a very important factor and distribution to anywhere in the country was possible. The article in Talking Machine World noted that Granby's "unexcelled facilities" for the production of phonographs in Newport News would prove to another great accomplishment for Newport News due to its location. The factory worked 24 hours a day during the early 1920's, allowing for multiple shifts and overtime. At this point in time, Harry Coplan was the Plant Manager and Edmond C. Howard was Sales Manager. The Factory Superintendent was Charles F. Pitt, Vice President of American Cabinet Manufacturing Corp. All official correspondence was directed to Norfolk, VA, the head of American Home Furnishers Corporation. Later, in 1922, all correspondence and was directed to the factory in Newport News.

On September 3, 1921, a new sign was installed on the Granby factory in Newport News. The sign read "The Home of the Granby Phonograph."[15] It was illuminated at night and could be seen by thousands of travelers along the Chesapeake and Ohio railroad coming and going to Newport News, VA. And, following in the footsteps of Harry Levy, Credit Manager Irving Beckhardt led a tour of fellow Kiwanis Club members through the factory in October of 1921. They were shown the way a "phonograph is supposed to made" and left with some souvenirs.[16]

---

[15] "New Sign on Granby Factory." TMW. 9-15-1921. Page 21.
[16] "New Granby Models Announced." TMW. 10-15-1921. Page 86.

The complex was built in phases. J. Davis built the original portion at a cost $20,000 and the second portion was built at a cost of $75,000. Later, in 1922, a permit was secured and construction was commenced on a four story wing that fronted Virginia Ave. at a cost of $70,000.00. J. Davis also built this wing and the job was finished in February of 1923. This completed the building as seen today.

(Left)   Construction of the new wing fronting Virginia Ave.

Talking Machine World

The Baltimore Connection

It is important to pause here and note the Baltimore connection. Only three of the 18 stores in the American Home Furnishers Corporation did not operate under the name Phillip Levy & Co. (as of 1922) They were Meyers & Tabakin of Norfolk, VA, Harlow-Willcox Co. of Petersburg, VA, and Pollack's of Baltimore, MD. Baltimore, MD featured two large warehouses for distribution and there is an account of a "branch furniture factory." This factory is highlighted in advertising and evidence shows, through modern day research, that this was a hub for Granby phonographs and furniture distribution.

This photograph shows a factory/warehouse in Baltimore. If you look closely, you can see a Pollack's truck backed up on the left and some furniture sitting outside on the right. The large painted sign says American Home Furnishers Corp. and the smaller white sign by the truck says American Cabinet Manufacturing Division.

46

An Introduction to Talking Machine World

Talking Machine World was a popular trade journal in the early twentieth century geared towards wholesalers and retailers of any kind of phonograph. It was *also* Granby's avenue to the national market. A large amount of this research came from The Talking Machine World and a complete bibliography is included for reference and continued reading. The Granby phonograph was formally introduced in August of 1920. Seven phonograph models were illustrated and an extensive advertising campaign was initiated, appealing to potential wholesalers and retailers. Not only did this marketing have to sell the product, but they had to sell the company *behind* the product so that retail businesses would feel comfortable with the relationship. Much of the language used and ads in this publication were geared towards *selling*. Simple headlines and updates on progress were meant to impress potential dealers.

Granby's ads answered questions and invited inquiries. Their September ad had 3 points of interest and highlighted what the Granby organization could provide:

1. An instrument that will compare to the best in the current field,

2. A close co-operation with wholesale and retail distributors who are "to share in the success" of Granby, including an "intense cultivation of local territories where Granby is presented," and

3. The financial resources to carry this program out; financial resources that do not depend on an overnight success.

Notice that Granby touts their connection with a large and established backing corporation without directly stating it. These three points assured the Granby dealer that the company would be by their side to aide them in marketing and this would lead to the ultimate success of the Granby in their respective businesses.

An October ad noted that "Granby craftsman are experts in their vocation, with so great a pride in their handiwork that nothing but a quality product could result." It must have been quite an honor working at the Granby factory in Newport News at this point in time to see that in writing. Another ad reads, "What the Granby selling franchise really means." In this ad, a four point summary is given on why the dealer should select the Granby to sell in their store(s). Furthermore, they state that their facilities "could not be improved upon" and high aspirations are apparent when the distributor is assured "prestige and profit and an indestructible asset in the Granby name and fame." Four elements of Granby strength are touted in the December ad; the character of Granby's

1. Product,

2. Factory producing that said product,

3. Their financial resources, and

4. Their selling co-operation.

"THIS IS THE LINE I WANT—THIS IS THE KIND OF DEALER SUPPORT THAT WILL IN-CREASE MY BUSINESS—YEAR AFTER YEAR"

Right now is the time to line up with this line. GET FULL DETAILS AT ONCE

GRANBY PHONOGRAPH CORPORATION

N O R F O L K - V I R G I N I A

·· Factory · Newport News ·· ·

An example of the type of language seen in Talking Machine World

This ad was seen in the October, 1920 edition

Granby's advertising (and confidence) was having its effect on the buying public. By October 2, 1920, Edmond C. Howard, the corporation's Sales Manager, was traveling around speaking with potential prospects and having success. Mr. Howard was instrumental in the inception of the Widdicomb Phonograph and the L'Artiste Phonograph product lines prior to joining Granby in August of 1920. He was described as a "great enthusiast and indefatigable worker" when it came to the phonograph industry. Photographs of E. C. Howard are rare due to his reluctance to get pictures taken after an incident occurred when a Chicago photographer lost the original "plates" but a photograph was finally obtained and can be seen herewith. It should be noted that Mr. Howard turned down several other job opportunities to take the position at Granby.[17]

Under his guidance, the company's exceptional cooperation extended to dealers was responsible for their success in establishing agents. Granby was, in turn, happy with the enthusiasm displayed by dealers. Ziegler, Baker, and Johnson, who were "well known in the eastern trade" according to Talking Machine World selected the Granby only after making a thorough investigation of its musical quality and studying the local market conditions. They reported that they were sure the Granby would be met with a large demand in the metropolis areas they served in the New York area.

On November 15th, A. J. Heath and Company of Philadelphia, who already distributed the Cirola Phonograph and Okeh Records, made an announcement about their Granby affiliation and their plans to grow and prosper. Heath's executive headquarters, storerooms, and record filing department were found in their "new quarters at 27 S.

---

[17] "Pays Tribute to Trade Paper." TMW. 9-15-1920. Page 203.

Seventh St. in Philadelphia, PA." A. J. Heath was President of the company and C. A. Malliet, formerly with Columbia Graphophone Co., was Vice President. The sales staff consisted of four men and was "expected to double." By now, the branch office in Baltimore had opened and served stores in that territory.

H. H. Shumaker, seen in this photograph, was Secretary and General Manager of American Home Furnishers Corporation. He was instrumental in establishing Granby in the Baltimore area.

In December, the Iroquois Sales Corporation of Buffalo, New York announced that they were going to start distributing the Granby. They were located at 10-14 North Division Street in Buffalo. Lionel M. Cole, Sales Manager, took an extensive trip through the territory with E. C. Howard of Granby to develop ideas for an intensive advertising campaign. Iroquois received attention for their trademark which was considered "ingenious" for the time period. The popular interpretation was that the illustration was an "Indian figure firmly planted on Buffalo no matter how fast he may gallop over the territory."

Granby was very proud of this affiliation and ran a full page ad in the December edition of Talking Machine World announcing the new relationship with Iroquois. Iroquois was quoted as saying that they "were tired of listening to mere promises and after a thorough investigation, we have secured the Granby franchise." Granby was on the way to becoming nationally known by this point in time in late 1920. Their beautiful phonographs and quality of sound production received attention. However, the marketing and unique advertising was *just beginning.*

Key Granby Distributors Gained in 1920

Name	Home Office	Territory Covered
A.J. Heath & Co.	Philadelphia, PA	Philadelphia, Eastern PA, Southern New Jersery, Delaware, Baltimore, Washington D.C.
Iroquois Sales Corp.	Buffalo, NY	Buffalo, New York area
R.J. Waters	Chicago, Ill.	Middle Western Franchise
R. Montalvo	New Brunswick, New Jersey	Northern New Jersey, also carried Granbys in his retail stores; New Brunswick, Perth Amboy, & Plainfield, NJ
Ziegler, Baker, & Johnson		New York Distributors

The 1920 Granby Catalog

Granby Phonograph Corporation soon started receiving attention for their printed work *in addition* to their phonographs. Their catalogs and other pieces of literature gained a reputation for their quality. Talking Machine World noted that catalogs by the phonograph industry were among the most attractive literature sent out by any industry but Granby's catalog represented the foremost in the field. The first catalog showing their complete line came off the press on September 15, 1920. It was "an excellent example of modern printing and engraving." The cover design was in the "pipes of pan" theme in pale green and white as the color selection. It featured a section that devoted equal time to each of the 8 phonographs that made up the Granby line. Details of the four consoles and four upright models were given concerning construction, finish, and features such as gold plated hardware and other details depending on the model. At the end of the catalog, a four page closing article discussed the "purpose of the Granby Phonograph Corp." In this section, the design, construction, and finish of the cabinets was discussed as well as the motor which they claimed would "become famous the world over." They conclude by stating "the most important feature of the Granby Phonograph can never be explained in a catalog" and "the test of time will show the owner of a Granby that the phonograph is a quality product, inside and out." The talking machine industry must have been quite taken by Granby's entrance into the market. The following quote speaks as a testament to that fact. The same "good taste with artistic perfection of the model designs of the Granby line is also represented in the printed presentation of the line."[18]

---

[18] "An Interesting Publication." TMW. 9-15-1920. Page 67.

One – Chippendale Console, Two – Queen Anne Console
Three – Queen Anne Upright, Four – Louis XVI Upright, Five – Adam Upright
Six – Adam Console, Seven – Louis XVI Console

The Granby line was *first* seen in a double page ad on August 15, 1920. A double page ad was taken out in both August and September. The new Granby's were said to be designed by "one of the foremost designers in Grand Rapids." *He or she was never named.* Of the eight models produced, seven were most often seen in ads during this period. The complete line consisted of four period "console" models and four period "upright" models, although only seven were shown. Consoles are low and wide cabinets and uprights are the common "Victrola" like phonographs with record storage *below* the amplifying horn.

Granby Phonographs featured elaborate woodwork which included curved or carved legs, unique veneer designs, and very detailed/elaborate grills (which covered the horn where the sound would come out). Unfortunately, many upright Granby phonographs found today have lost their original grills due to damage or because of customization by owners throughout the 1950's to 1990's. Wood accents varied depending on model. Prices ranged from $140.00 to $325.00. Upright Granby Phonographs can be recognized by the patented curved top of the lid. Also, Granby Phonographs have an identification plate on the rear of the cabinet which contains the Granby logo and a "case number." *Early* Leviolas and Granbys do not feature the curved top and identification tag on the rear of the cabinet.

Harry Levy was remembered by his daughter as a man of extremely good taste and this is apparent in the Granby Phonograph line and its presentation. These phonographs were, no doubt, almost *upscale* in the way they were advertised. Unlike the local advertising in Newport News seen in the Daily Press, *national* ads in Talking Machine World featured unique models with the new trademark features that bared no resemblance to the left over Leviolas.

Granby Phonographs Announced in 1920

Only seven were seen in the introductory ad in Talking Machine World

The Sheraton Model seen below was a great seller but seldom seen in **early** advertisements.

Queen Anne Console	Queen Anne Upright
Adam Console	Adam Upright
Louis XVI Console	Louis XVI Upright
Chippendale Console	Sheraton (No. 13) Upright

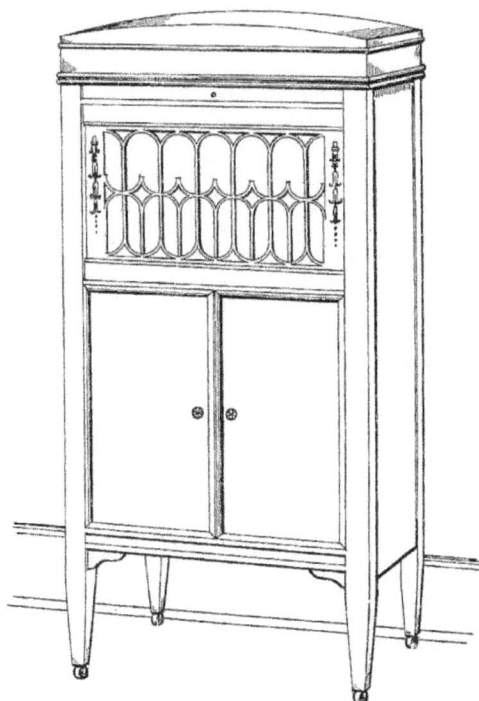

Inventor
E C HOWARD
By his Attorney
George C. Dean

E. C. Howard's Patent drawing of the Sheraton Upright (No. 13)

Application Filed October 14, 1920 and Granted on May 17, 1921

The Granby Proposition

Granby impressed the phonograph industry again in November of 1920. Here, Granby was said "to be a firm believer in the power of the printed word in artistic dress" by Talking Machine World. The piece of literature that was getting attention was "The Granby Proposition." This "superbly printed volume" was supplementary to the catalog and the cover was gold and red. It was geared toward potential dealers of the Granby line and outlined,

1. Promises and performance,

2. The Granby Institution,

3. The Granby Phonograph,

4. Equipment, and

5. Real co-operation with the Distributor and Retailer.

The Proposition stated that no national advertising campaign was planned but a local newspaper campaign could be initiated depending on,

1. The number of prospects,

2. The initial purchase by the said dealer, and

3. The amount of business developed by the dealer in conjunction with the campaign.

This certainly came as no surprise. Harry Levy was an innovator in, and strong believer in, the power of newspaper advertising. This was evident in Phillip Levy & Co.'s history and presence in the local paper. He could almost *create* his own headlines and make product introductions seem like quite an event. A perfect example is how the Leviola was introduced and marketed back in 1919. According to the Granby Proposition, it was obvious that this principle and concept was integrated into the Granby business model.

The Granby Proposition also outlined and provided a summary of material that would be furnished to the dealers. This material included catalogs, folders, window displays, and rotogravure cards which would show each Granby Phonograph in the *properly* furnished room. These cards were meant to be an aide to potential purchasers of the Granby. Illustrations and a "bird's eye" view of the factory in Newport News were pictured, as well. The Proposition also announced a new monthly publication that Granby would publish and send out called *Melodie.*

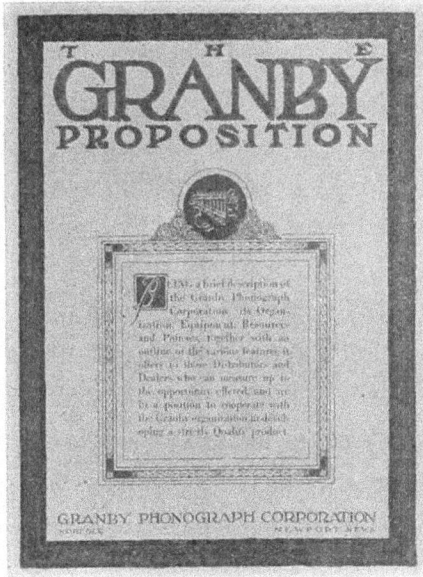

In November, the first issue of Melodie came off the press! It was a monthly publication that Granby Phonograph Corporation distributed to dealers in quantity according to their mailing lists. Melodie was devoted to "all things musical." Also, it was specifically designed as a marketing tool to keep Granby phonographs on the mind of the public. Talking Machine World noted that it was "consistent with other high quality Granby literature." It was eight pages long and printed on "super quality" stock with "careful selection of type and harmonious blending of colors." It was said to be "attractive to a high degree." The opening article in the first edition was devoted to Antonio Stradivari and his great accomplishments. Other articles on folk songs, modern musical instruments, and the power of music were also present. The publication ended with suggestions for record purchases in a section called "recent records worth while."[19]

---

[19] "Latest Granby Literature." TMW. 11-15-20. Page 97.

In December, the "rotogravure" mailing cards that were mentioned in The Granby Proposition started receiving attention in the phonograph industry. Rotogravure is a printing process in which an image is engraved/etched on a large cylinder and then printed. It became popular in the early 20th century because of its use by the newspaper industry partly because of the great quality of images and text that could be produced. Granby's rotogravure cards measured 4 by 6 inches and were meant to aid the customer in selecting the right Granby for their home. The cards were meant to be used by dealers for their "first class prospects." On each card, one of the eight Granby phonographs was shown in the surroundings in which it harmonized with. The back of the card featured a small amount of text about the phonograph pictured. Talking Machine World noted that the cards were "extremely attractive" and could "practically serve the purpose of the interior decorator" in addition to the selection of the correct phonograph for the home. *Once again*, the upscale marketing and Harry Levy's good taste were apparent. Granby phonographs were not meant to be confused with *bargain* phonographs.

In addition to the printed work, there was another item of interest that was sent to Granby dealers. Two "artistic panels" that featured the Granby slogan, "as mellow as southern moonlight" were meant to be placed on the walls of dealers' showrooms. The panels featured southern moonlight scenes in which the Granby phonograph was featured. These were certainly designed for a *prominent* spot on the wall of a Granby showroom.

In summary, the later part of 1920 was spent selling off Leviola style phonographs in the Newport News market and securing wholesalers and retailers in the national market. Phillip Levy & Co. of Norfolk, VA sold 421 Granby phonographs in December of 1920 because of "intensive selling, backed by constant newspaper advertising" according to a January, 1921 article in Talking Machine World. While selling, considerable time was also spent on designing a distinct product, with unique features, and creating a marketing plan that would benefit the Granby dealer which would benefit the Granby Phonograph Corporation in the long run. The phonographs were classy and attention to detail was apparent. Granby's plan of close co-operation with dealers and their supporting materials which included catalogs, mailing cards, sales folders, and artistic signs for showrooms would prove to be very impressive to dealers. As Granby looked toward 1921, the company was preparing to take the phonograph industry by storm.

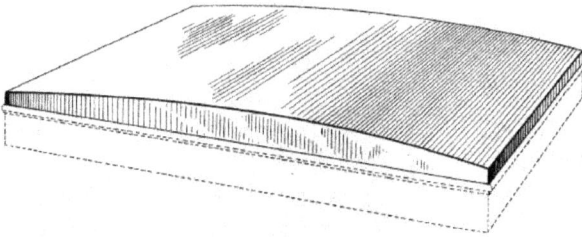

E. C. Howard's Patent drawing of Granby Phonograph's Dome Lid

And Tone Arm

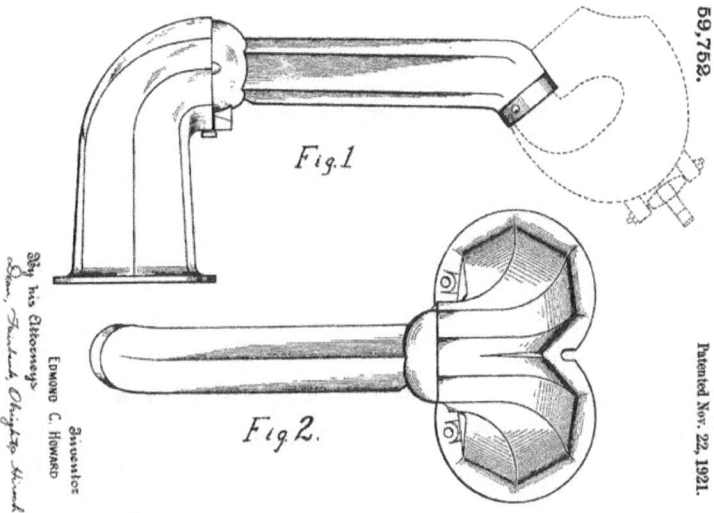

PART III: 1921

The Year of the Granby

Building a Network

As the New Year rang in, Harry Levy and the American Home Furnishers Corporation, were going strong. They used the previous retail season's impressive sales figures in advertising to prove that the Granby was appealing to the public. Much of 1921 was spent securing new dealers for the Granby line and E. C. Howard, Sales Manager, was doing a fine job. New wholesalers like A. J. Heath and Iroquois were out obtaining new retail outlets, as well. On March 8th, L. M. Cole of Iroquois announced that Howard and Winslow, Inc. of Middletown, NY and Hills, McLean, and Haskins of Binghamton, NY had come aboard. During this period in time, billboard ads for Granby

Phonographs could be seen in Middletown. A March 27th ad was placed in the New York Times showing the model line and the names of dealers. By April, a warehouse was established in New York City with M. Milton Roemer as the distributor, who supplied over 40 Granby dealers. Mr. Roemer had previously distributed Vitanola phonographs and knew the market well.

The month of April was spent making one announcement after another of new Granby dealers. A. I. Namm and Son, one of Brooklyn's leading department stores, as well as Federal Phonograph Co. of Pittsburgh, PA were among the new dealers. On the home front in Virginia, exciting things were happening, also. The Hotel Warwick in Newport News hosted a monthly gathering of Granby workers. A dinner was given by factory management to its foreman as a "stimulus to production and an opportunity to discuss conditions throughout the plant."[20] Also, growing sales were apparent when A. J. Heath & Co. announced that April sales were better than March.

Granby Phonographs Sold on Exceptionally Liberal Terms to Reliable People

Federal Talking Machine Co.

3009 Jenkins Arcade (3rd Floor)

Good Territory Open to Wideawake Dealers.

The Granby Phonograph is made at Newport News, Virginia—in a plant with an equipment second to none in the world in quality—by an organization of master craftsmen made possible by an institution of ample financial resources.

The Pittsburgh Press, Sunday, March 13, 1921

By May, Iroquois Sales Corporation had settled into their new quarters on the fourth floor of the King and Eisele Building in Buffalo, NY. This came at a pivotal time because this new location allowed the Granbys to be well displayed. Granby phonographs seemed to be

---

[20] "Dinner Given to Granby Force". TMW. 4-15-1921. Page 77.

going lots of places. For example, on May 2nd, it was announced that a Granby would be going to *India*. It seemed that Rev. and Mrs. Goedke, missionaries to India, purchased a Queen Anne model to take with them on their travels.

Another important announcement was made on June 5, 1921 that would greatly help the Granby phonograph distribution. The Talking Machine World called it "one of the most important announcements in recent history of the talking machine trade." A deal had been struck between Harry Levy – President, H.H. Schumaker – Secretary, E. C. Howard – Sales Director, and James G. Widener of Widener's Inc. The deal stated that Mr. Widener, who operated a chain of 14 department stores, based in Boston, would take on the Granby line and sell them through all of his stores.[21] His stores also carried Columbia Grafonolas. 9 of the 14 Widener's retail locations would serve as wholesale distribution points due to their geographic location. This deal had been in the negotiating and planning stages for some time. Mr. Schumaker had visited several of Widener's important stores and Mr. Widener had inspected the Granby factory in person. It should be noted that this deal did not disturb the national distribution agreement that Granby already had with the Kennedy-Schultz Co. of Cleveland and Iroquois Sales Corp. of Buffalo, NY. They continued as "jobbing representatives."

Both parties to this agreement were satisfied with the other. Harry Levy and James Widener could certainly see "eye to eye" being that they both operated a chain of retail stores. They understood what each other needed and expected to make the venture successful. This particular announcement is one of only a few times that Harry Levy's name would come up on the national platform in Talking Machine World. Previous and future announcements came from E. C. Howard, Harry Coplan, or one of their many salesman. A letter sent by James G. Widener from Boston to the Granby HQ in Norfolk, VA explains his happiness with Granby.

---

[21] "Granby Line in Widener's Stores." TMW. 6-15-21. Page 50.

"We have searched the field for months and have gone over all talking machines, endeavoring to find something to fit what we needed most, viz: First, an instrument that would give our customers satisfaction; second, a tone the majority would like; third, an instrument that would keep our time accounts using and paying on them; fourth, one that would give least mechanical troubles, fifth, an instrument from a furniture standpoint that would fit into the majority of homes. After six months exhaustive study we have found it – the Granby."

Signed J. G. Widener, President

The Peak of Perfection in Phonographs —THE GRANBY

July Records Now on Sale

Introductory Offer

Try Before You Buy

After an extensive investigation and comparison with all other makes—we have selected the

Granby Phonograph

as the best instrument for our customers

Everything You Have Wanted in a Phonograph —And More

—the beautiful Granby tone, as clear and mellow as a violin.

—the artistic Granby cabinet, made by the finest furniture craftsmen in the country.

—and you can play all records on the Granby.

Pay No Money Down

Let us send a Granby to your home without obligation. Play it for a reasonable time. Study the Granby from every viewpoint. If you decide to buy, we will arrange very convenient purchase terms.

This offer for a limited time only.

Widener's

1008 Olive St.

If You Cannot Call, 'Phone Main 2877.

Granby Phonographs

Columbia Grafonolas

Inspection in No Way Implies Purchase

St. Louis Post Dispatch

Thursday, June 16, 1921

St. Louis, Missouri

63

Notice the reference to *time accounts*. This *proves* that Mr. Levy and Mr. Widener had something in common. American Home Furnishers Corporation had built their business model on the installment business. For example, a 1923 financial statement showed that 3.5 million dollars of American Home Furnishers 5.2 million dollars in working assets were in *accounts receivable*. Robert D. Duffy, who worked at the Widener's location in Indianapolis noted that the Granby's moderate price was good for smaller dealers, also. He had previously worked at Columbia Graphophone Co. as a Sales Manager and had an eye for market conditions and price points. His opinion was that smaller dealers couldn't afford to put too much money in inventory that would return "too little on profit."

During this period, other "jobbing representatives" were doing well, also. Edward L. Ginsburg, factory salesman was appointed to Iroquois Sales Corporation at this point in time to assist in their needs and on June 5, 1921 ordered three carloads of Granbys. That is *train* car loads…

By July, Harry Coplan was now on the road doing quite a bit of sales work. The factory back home in Newport News was rolling and he felt needed elsewhere. On July 3rd, he was working in Ohio with the Kennedy-Schultz Company, newly appointed distributors for that territory. The company was operated by H. C. Schultz and Charles H. Kennedy, whose offices where on the fourth floor of the Newman-Stern Building in Cleveland. They previously were Columbia Grafonola dealers and knew their territory well. All dealers served by the Kennedy-Schultz Co. received electric signs for their storefront windows showing the Granby trademark. Their warehouse in Cleveland featured a service and refinishing department so the machines would be in "tip top" shape before going out to retailers. An interesting article appeared in Talking Machine World during this period in which Mr. Harry Coplan is described as "one of the newest people to the phonograph trade but one of the oldest of the American Home Furnishers Corp, the parent company to Granby." This article was run while Mr. Coplan was in Ohio saying that he could be considered a specialist in the installment business and in summary, did his job well. Interestingly, the article did not note that the phonograph factory was *his* idea from the start...

While Harry Coplan was working away in Ohio, Consolidated Talking Machine Company of Chicago announced that they had taken on the Granby line. They would represent Granby in Illinois, Michigan, and Southern Wisconsin as a wholesale distributor. E. L. Ginsburg, Assistant Sales Manager at Granby helped in the closing of the deal. Consolidated Talking Machine Co. intended to place the Granby in every store possible that it served from its Chicago and Detroit branches. Granby was gaining quite a reputation at this time because this announcement referred to the phonograph "one of the best known of the newer makes of talking machines." Newspaper ads were being run constantly in local markets and the Granby was getting great press in Talking Machine World since their entrance into the national market in August of 1920.

More Workers... and More Buildings

By July 7th, 100 skilled workers had been added to the workforce by this time which was "materially increasing its daily production" in Newport News. Because of this fact, Granby leased the Pabst Building on 26th Street between Virginia Ave. and the railroad, across the street from their factory. This building got used at a "stock assembly plant." The corporation also secured the Royal Warehouse and the second floor of the Holloway Building on 25th Street. In addition to the new space, Granby had to tear out areas that were previously used as offices in order to be used for phonograph production.

The extra space was definitely needed because, by this point in time, Granby phonographs were being sold in many big distributing centers of the country. Talking Machine World noted that their sales records attested to their popularity and that "the excellent workmanship which characterizes this product" accounted for its steadily rising popularity. This was great progress for a company just over one year in the national phonograph business.

The August issue of Talking Machine World introduced Granby's Credit Manager, Irving Beckhardt. He was described as a man of "exceptional ability" and became associated with the company in its very beginning. Mr. Beckhardt originally worked as an Auditor with the company and at this point was purchasing all raw and finished material for the factory. The position of Credit Manager was very important with a large organization like Granby. He also had charge of all of the finances of American Cabinet Manufacturing Corporation which was allied with the Granby Corporation. Described as being "one of the leading officials of the organization," he graduated from the College of the City of New York. Talking Machine World described him as a typical executive of the growing corporation.[22] As previously noted, he was a member of the Kiwanis.

---

[22] "Beckhardt New Credit Manager." TMW. 8-15-1921. Page 26.

Everything may have been fine with Harry Coplan and Irving Beckhardt but there were some other personnel issues brewing. Edmond C. Howard, Director of Sales, had gone on vacation back on July 19th. On a humorous side note, he ultimately returned with a new car although he did not have a driver's license. Either there were some indications of a problem or maybe Granby thought that he would *find himself* while on his break. Whatever the cause, they did not wait for him to resign. Granby moved forward with hiring Edward Fraser Carson *in his absence* during August and gave him the title of Assistant General Manager. Pictured on the left, Mr. Carson had previously served as Manager of the copy and plan department of an advertising agency in New York City. He was given complete charge of the Advertising and Sales Department at Granby, although his official title was Assistant General Manager.

Upon Mr. Howard's return from his vacation, the official announcement of his resignation came on September 1, 1921. Either Mr. Howard *planned* to resign or he was upset by the hiring of Mr. Carson. Either way, his resignation was final and this was a blow to the company. E. C. Howard was pivotal and responsible for much of the growth of Granby in its early days. He was also very respected and admired in the talking machine trade. Many patents put forth for the early Granby cabinet designs and features bore Mr. Howard's signature. Mr. Howard left Norfolk on October 1st with his wife and daughter, Janet. They went to Grand Rapids and then made their way his home of Oakland, California. During this transitionary time, Harry

67

Coplan stepped in and inherited some of E. C. Howard's former job duties and gained the job title, "Field Sales Manager."

Crawford T. Westmoreland, seen in this photo, was Factory Superintendent during this period. Formerly of High Point, NC and having been in the work working field for over 27 years, Mr. Westmoreland had an impressive resume. He designed several of the period models in the Granby line-up and became affectionately known as "Dad" around the factory. When there was an issue, the comment could be heard, "ask Dad… he knows."[23] Things were obviously in good hands in Newport News so Mr. Coplan got busy preparing for the fall campaign and checked in with Widener's and Iroquois Sales Corp.

In October, Rene Jaccard, final inspector at the Granby Factory, had just returned from his "flying visit" to New York. Mr. Jaccard was 25 years old in 1921 and had immigrated to America from Switzerland. He previously lived in Ohio prior to moving to Newport News. Also, during this time, Irving Beckhardt had just underwent a surgery to remove an abcess that resulted from an old injury. As reported by Talking Machine World, the surgery put an end to the trouble.

---

[23] "A Real Fountain of Knowedge…" TMW. 9-15-1921. Page 42.

In October, Granby announced the hiring of Oramel P. Graffen who was well known in New York phonograph and business circles. His job was to represent Granby in New York City and the larger cities in New Jersey. He was under the direction of R. R. Wilson, who was the New York sales representative of the Granby line. Mr. Graffen brought with him experience totaling nearly 16 years. 14 of those years were spent with the well-known Columbia Graphophone Co. and 2 years were spent at Victor Talking Machine Co.[24]

Granby phonographs were shown at the Ohio Convention of Music Dealers that was held September 12th through the 14th. Charles H. Kennedy and H. C. Schultz were in charge of the exhibit. This *certainly* helped Granby's exposure in that territory and on October 5th, Granby announced two new models – one upright and one console. The upright, seen on the right, was known as the No. 10 Sheraton and listed at $100.00. It was offered in the choice of mahogany, walnut, or oak. The console was given the No. 50 and was *also* known as the Sheraton. The price was $175.00. Unlike the upright Sheraton, it was not offered in the oak option. Remember, there was another Sheraton already in the Granby

line. That particular upright Sheraton was part of the original lineup of eight and not emphasized in *early* advertisements. However, although not emphasized, the entry level Sheraton models were great sellers! Ads appearing in Talking Machine World during this period directed

---

[24] "O. P. Graffen with Granby Corp." TMW. 10-15-21. Page 37.

all correspondence to Norfolk, VA, specifically the Levy Building. Ads urged potential customers to join the "Granby Army of Merchants."

The Sheraton Model 50 Console

Queen Anne Upright

It is Surprising

upon what moderate terms you can install the graceful

GRANBY
PHONOGRAPH.

in your home.

Many of your neighbors are buying this quality instrument.

Made in Period Styles. Plays all records *much better.*

Come in. See it. Hear it.

Priced $100
and Up

Terms to Suit

BUETTNER
FURNITURE CO.

N. E. Cor. Eighth and Washington

Granby Day

One very memorable marketing event that occurred in the history of Granby Phonograph Corporation happened on October 16, 1921 in St. Louis. The day was dubbed "Granby Day." Newspapers ran large Granby ads and all of the furniture stores that had taken on the Granby line featured elaborate window displays. Mr. E. W. Schumaker, who represented the Granby in St. Louis is credited with all the hard work of securing the new dealers that necessitated this event. *(not to be confused with H. H. Schumaker who resided in Norfolk, VA)* Dealers that participated in this event were Buettner Furniture Co., Widener's Inc., H. F. Geitz Co., David's Furniture Co., Tower Music Shoppe, and Deeken Music Co.

Business was booming for Granby. On November 1st, Granby announced the factory would be enlarged. Remember, the corporation had already leased additional warehouse space. Mr. Beckhardt and Mr. Westmoreland investigated factories all over the country to decide on what concept would be most advantageous. Obviously, many furniture factories were observed including locations in North Carolina, Cincinnati, Louisville, Michigan, and New England. Even Mr.

F. W. Connelly of the Philadelphia office made a trip down to the Newport News factory to check out what was going on. During his time in Virginia, he traveled around checking out the major cities where the Granby was being sold and marketed. He, no doubt, visited the Phillip Levy & Co. stores in Newport News, Norfolk, Richmond and others.

December of 1921 brought even more marketing concepts. One instance was found at S. Steinbrecher's establishment which was located at 1850-52-54 Ridge Ave. in Philadelphia, PA. Being that he was a Granby dealer and nearly 100 cars passed by his store *every* hour, he decided to put a sign on his store, but not just *any* sign. This was a very, *very* large sign that earned attention in Talking Machine World. Supposedly the sign drew so much interest that his store got very crowded and he needed several delivery trucks to keep up with deliveries. Talking Machine World referred to him as "a hustler."[25]

---

[25] "Granby Quaker City Dealer." TMW. 12-15-21. Page 22.

A photograph of Mr. Steinbrecher's store seen in Talking Machine World

And, if Granby Day seemed like an event to behold, that was nothing compared to what Speare Music Company in Dover, Ohio did on Halloween. The store put on a Halloween Party and the honored guest was *Virginia Granby* who was impersonated by one of the prominent young ladies of the city. She made her way around town and nobody could identify her which created quite a mystery.

In the city's Halloween Parade, the Speare Music Co. created a float devoted to Granby which won third place in more than 90 floats that participated. A structure in the front of the float carried the Granby slogan "As Mellow as Southern Moonlight" showing through a door with moonlight flowing through. A *spotlight* was the source of the moonlight. Several Granbys were placed on the float and played throughout the parade. Virginia Granby was seated on the front of the float next to one of the instruments and H. C. Schultz dressed up as George Washington. This must have been quite a sight to see! The mission was achieved and Granby received lots publicity from this event.

Another instance involving a parade occurred when the Granby phonograph was introduced at J. H. Johnson and Sons in Alliance, Ohio. The store held a parade to announce the Granby in which banners were shown and literature was handed out. Prior to that, telegrams were placed in the window stating that the Granby was on its way. People did not even know it was a phonograph until it arrived on opening day. Newspaper circulation jumped from 18,000 to 45,000 for the event. Other merchants in the area also held specials and an automobile was given away.

What began as Granby Day in St. Louis carried well into December thanks to the creativity of Granby wholesalers and retailers. The momentum gathered by these marketing events was capitalized on by Granby and its dealers. Of course, all this creativity was in addition to the old tried and true advertising that worked for Phillip Levy & Co. – *intense, nonstop, newspaper advertising in all local markets where Granby was sold.*

Unfortunately, this photograph isn't too clear, but it is the only known picture of the "Great Parade in honor of the Granby Phonograph in Alliance, Ohio"

Talking Machine World

Newspaper Advertising in Newport News, VA

Although Granby was gaining a national distribution network by this point in time, nothing much had changed in who sold the Granby phonographs back home. Phillip Levy & Co. was the Granby dealer for Newport News and Norfolk, VA. The Phillip Levy & Co. store in Newport News was located at 2508 Washington Avenue and the Norfolk store was located at the corner of Main and Church streets in Norfolk. (There were eight Phillip Levy retail locations and the Granby phonograph was sold in all of them.) Fergusson's, located at 2909-11 Washington Ave. in Newport News and Cheyne's Studio in Hampton sold the Victor Victrola. Fergusson Music Co. was quite a well-known music house in the country. Mr. Wallace W. Lanier was in charge of the phonograph and small goods department. Newport News Furniture Company sold the Columbia Grafonola and there was also a separate store on nearby Jefferson Avenue called The Grafonola Shop which exclusively sold the Columbia product. The Roundtree-Tennis Furniture Company in Hampton, VA sold Brunswick Phonographs and records later in 1924.

75

Some stores did sell "off brand" phonographs but none were as *heavily* promoted in the local area as the Granby. The nearest manufactured phonograph being offered at a Newport News store was the A. J. Crafts phonograph which was made in Richmond, VA. They were piano makers who had decided to get into the phonograph business and advertised in Talking Machine World. The Franklin phonograph of Philadelphia was also seen advertised in the Newport News and Hampton area in the early 1920's.

Phillip Levy & Co. advertised the Granby well in comparison to the other dealers. A phonograph was a hot item in the early 1920's locally, as well as nationwide. It was important to keep a presence in the newspaper and fulfill their promise of an intense advertising campaign as they mentioned in their literature geared towards wholesalers and retailers.

The Daily Press, Saturday, November 19, 1921

Newport News, Virginia

The trend in the phonograph industry was heavy newspaper advertising and sales were at their highest around the Christmas retail season. A gradual build up occurred in September through October of 1921. Unlike the previous Christmas season where the Granby phonographs looked very much like Leviolas, 1921 brought ads with true Granby phonographs featuring the domed lid and distinct features seen in Talking Machine World and patented by Mr. Howard. Prior to the Christmas season of 1921, Granby ads were usually mixed into a larger ad for all of Phillip Levy & Co.'s other furniture offerings that included rugs, stoves, and dining room sets. However, as Christmas drew closer, separate Granby ads that ran apart from the Phillip Levy & Co. furniture ads started being seen. Small vertical ads were sporadically placed in the newspaper. These smaller sized ads got right to the point. Features such as the Granby's "rich tone," free records, and the fact that the Granby played *all* records were emphasized.

Other full size ads ran with ornate and artistic renderings of the Granby on the top of the ad, accompanied by the Granby logo. On the bottom of the ad, the Phillip Levy & Co. name was inserted and centered, with Granby logos on each side. The main body of the ad contained a sales pitch for the Granby. These illustrations certainly give an insight into the quality of print that Granby was using for their rotogravure cards, catalogs, and *Melodie* magazine. The ads were quite large and had a great presence in the newspaper.

The ads seemed like an organized template with uniform characteristics during this period. Inserting different stores names at the bottom would have been an easy task in different markets. The branding and advertising seemed organized. On November 9th, an ad ran that asked the customers to "choose the Granby by both your ear and eye." The ad emphasized tone and construction. The first payment of $5.00 was noted and credit would be extended to "out of town folks" who could write for a catalog if they wished. Phillip Levy & Co. told that they would "pay the freight."

Using the same template, "the Granby phonograph and what it means to children" was a concept that was advertised.[26] The ad cited the National Child Welfare Association and explained that a Granby would make the home a most popular place in the neighborhood and a place that "young folks can gather." It noted that "scientists tell us a love of music can be absorbed just as the body absorbs air and sunlight" and the Granby, which was finished to match the furniture in the customer's home, would add to the "character of the growing child and help him develop." Another ad followed up on the appeal of keeping the children at home. Again the National Child Welfare Association was cited in the fact that supper was very important family time. "Having a Granby in the home will keep the children at home." The concept was that keeping the children at home, listening to the Granby, would be a better alternative than having the young folks go out on the town, not to be seen again until the next morning.

Some ads also catered to the housewife. "Happy is the woman who does her housework to the cheerful tunes of the Granby" is the heading seen in a November 19th ad. When the husband was off to work and children at school is when the lady would get her enjoyment from the Granby. The ad further noted that Granby owners enjoy their home life in "a manner that can't be measured in dollars and cents." Music is said to strengthen and beautify life. The Granby, with its new and patented features would also benefit the father by helping him relax after a hard days' work. According to the ad, the phonograph could play 6 to 8 records once would up with the crank.

Granby was appealing to the entire family unit in this advertising campaign. The lady of the house, the father, and the children would receive benefits from a Granby phonograph in the house. This was traditional marketing at its best. To put things in perspective, these ads were appearing in 1921, just one year after women were granted the right to vote in America.

---

[26] November 24, 1921. Daily Press. Ad.

**After Supper, WHAT THEN?
MUSIC on the GRANBY unites
the Family in a Common Interest**

The very minute that grown boy or young lady in your home has eaten supper—the thought of "something to do for the evening" flashes thru their mind—a real test half-minute in deciding—up town boy the evening and you don't see them until morning.

Music on the beautiful Granby Phonograph will help to keep your children at home—the very fact that there is something to do after supper, music in their ears, home—radio invites them to entertain their friends at home—because there is something to hear, to behold just said.

All the famous musical artists of the world, the best military bands and proper jazz orchestras, can be brought to your home through music on the Granby phonograph that will please the tired business man, or invalids and soothe their tired nerves at the same time.

Those few hours after supper are important ones as far as the home is concerned. Music on the Granby will please you—please their friends and then too, music is the one thing that unites the entire family in a common interest and makes the home ties more lasting.

The Granby Phonograph Plays All Records

Granby records and Victrola records which are most all the music, as well as Victor, Columbia, Edison, Pathe and all other records, can all be played on the Granby without changing tone arms or using attachments.

Granby Phonographs are made in different period designs and are high in order to suit the taste of most homes. Come in now and hear the latest tabu in tone thru the exquisite "New Granby."

10 Selections Free!

Just to prove to you that the Granby Phonograph is worthy of a place in your home, we offer you ten double faced up-to-the-minute records absolutely free with each Granby—and remember in...

$1 Down

**Puts a Beautiful Granby Phonograph
In Your Home - Hear It Play - Today**

There are several good makes in this phonograph selling now—Just come in and pay your one dollar cash and have placed in your home—Pay the balance in easy payments.

PHILLIP LEVY & CO. DIV.

The Daily Press, Thursday, March 10, 1921

79

The Granby Christmas Club

The Christmas season of 1921 saw the return of the Granby Christmas Club, a concept that had also been used in 1920. The Christmas Club wasn't unique to the Granby phonograph. Phillip Levy & Co. also utilized the concept with lamps and stoves. The Christmas Club was formally started on November 1st. With the Granby Christmas Club, an individual would pay just 40 cents and that would guarantee the Granby be delivered on Christmas Day. The customer would be allowed 40 musical sections free of charge as part of the promotion. That came in the form of 20 double sided 78 rpm records valued at 85 cents. A 67 week payment plan would follow the initial payment with the highest payment being $1.85 at one point.[27] It was stated that the home on Christmas morning with "a Granby phonograph in the corner would be one of the happiest homes in the city." It is interesting to note a block of text that was seen in these ads that stated "your old worn out phonograph accepted as part payment on a new Granby."

A Letter from Harry Levy

As previously discussed, Harry Levy would do "letter style" ads that touched on various subjects from why furniture prices were up, down, or the Granby phonograph. These "letter style" ads would be the size of a standard medium sized ad commonly seen in the newspaper. One particular letter stands out because of the open discussion of the Granby phonograph. The title was "making it easy to give a phonograph" and told what Phillip Levy & Co. did to make it easier for a working person to obtain a phonograph. He summarized by stating that payments could be made "next year, in weekly or monthly payments as you feel you can afford."[28] This personal appeal and helpful demeanor separated Harry Levy from the rest. Even though the letter stated otherwise, payments were *usually* structured.

---

[27] November 9, 1921. Daily Press. Ad.
[28] December 16, 1921. Daily Press. Ad.

If you were not participating in the Christmas Club, you could expect to pay the standard $5.00 down and $2.00 per week after that. As previously offered in 1920, 10 free records would still come with the purchase of a new Granby. And, as before, Granby was being careful not to be confused with "bargain" or "close-out" phonographs. They noted that "the Granby phonograph is being made today in our own factory." This was a slight change from previous years in that now, they plainly stated they owned the factory.

As 1921 drew to a close, Phillip Levy & Co. would do whatever it took to place the phonograph in the home of everybody, no matter what your social position, and they offered the "in house" credit program to back up their offers. As seen, the child, housewife, and father could stand to benefit. Harry Levy wrote letters, initiated a Christmas Club, and kept a presence in the newspaper. All of this was occurring while Edward F. Carson and other executives of the company were designing new ads and making new contacts on the national level, trying to achieve even *more* success during 1922.

Key Wholesale Distribution Points Gained During 1921

Name	Home Office	Territory Covered
Consolidated Talking Machine Co.	Chicago, Ill.	Illinois, Michigan, Southern Wisconsin
Granby Office & Warehouse M. Milton Roemer, Distributor	New York City	Supplied over 40 dealers in the NY area
Kennedy-Schultz Co.	Cleveland, Ohio	Northern Ohio
Widener's Inc.	Boston, Mass	9 of the 14 stores were designated as wholesale distributing points

New Granby Sheraton Phonographs Announced in 1921

No. 10 Sheraton Upright	No. 50 Sheraton Console
Price $ 100.00	Price $175.00
Available in Mahogany, Oak, Walnut	Available in Mahogany and Walnut

PART IV: 1922

Steady Growth... from Phonographs to Furniture

An American Home Furnishers delivery truck departs a Norfolk, Virginia warehouse stocked with furniture circa 1922 – 23.

Christopher James Stoessner Collection

Encouraging Reports

On Janurary 3, 1922, Mr. L. M. Lytton of Burgettstown, PA, had a unique idea on how to sell the Granby. He placed a Granby console on the rear of his Ford and drove down mud roads to get to the mining communities. He would then make a sales pitch about the higher priced Granby console. One could only imagine seeing a Ford driving down a country road with a big Granby console sitting in the back. The article concludes, "he wastes no time in his store." Like Mr. Steinbrecher in Philadelphia, it appeared that there was another "hustler."

On January 3, Granby was receiving encouraging reports from all its dealers in the country. Mr. F. Connely, who was representing Granby in the Carolina region and making his headquarters in High Point, had recently been elected as an honorary member of the High Point Chamber of Commerce. Mr. Connely also announced that the Granby would affiliate with the Shipman Organ Company of High Point during this time. This helped Granby's exposure in the south.

Other progress was noted when it was announced by Mr. E. W. Shumaker that business was showing an improvement in the west and that more Granby dealers were being added in his territory. This is true because modern day research does show an abundance of ads present in Missouri area newspapers during this time period, second only to Virginia and the Northeast. Austin Fordham, representative of Granby in Eastern Pennsylvania also reported good news and noted that the "period design" Granbys were selling especially well.[29]

The Kennedy-Schultz Co., representing the Granby in the Ohio section reported the opening of another new store by the name of Frey-Fisher Co. Like other retailers, they chose to get creative with their marketing and hung more than 10,000 door knob hangers in the vicinity of the store to announce its opening.[30]

---

[29] "Recent Granby Activities." TMW. January 15, 1922. Page 26.
[30] "Granby Signs on Door Knobs." TMW. 1-15-22. Page 76.

Granby Sales Offices Move to Boston

A major announcement came on January 27th. The Granby Phonograph Corporation's main sales offices were being moved to 21 West Street in Boston, Mass. Edward F. Carson, who had been Assistant General Manager of the company for 8 months, was excited about the move and *probably* behind it. He noted, "for a long time the company felt that it was somewhat handicapped by operating from a general sales office located so far south." Harry Levy and other officials at American Home Furnishers Corporation probably raised an eyebrow at this comment. Keep in mind that the Granby was marketed as a phonograph with tone "as mellow as Southern moonlight."

Whatever the motivation, and whoever was *truly* behind it, the move went quickly. General Sales Offices closed in Norfolk on Saturday, January 14 and continued Monday, January 16th in Boston. Executive offices that housed the main officers of the company remained in Norfolk with Hugo H. Shumaker in charge. The factory remained in Newport News and no changes occurred there. However, all ads during this time said nothing about Norfolk or Newport News. The large font, "GRANBY PHONOGRAPH CORPORATION" was followed by "21 West Street - Boston, Mass." It definitely appeared that Granby was going for a different look. Maybe they really were tired of being the "southern" company in a northern industry. Or, maybe this was Mr. Carson's grand idea. *Only time would tell.*

Granby was also in the process of completing plans to expand the factory to accommodate the growing business the company anticipated for 1922. Harry Coplan, general sales manager, remained on the road touring territories where the Granby was represented, which was at this particular time, *Ohio*.

Mr. Carson was certainly enjoying his new role in the phonograph industry. March issues of Talking Machine World featured a monthly column written by Edward Carson. He covered such issues as "Promptness" and "Selfishness" in what appeared to be his take on the proper way to act and succeed in business. Nowhere in the heading did it say that he was Asst. Gen. Manager of Granby, which marketed itself as "the most profitable phonograph line in the industry" by this point in time. That only deserves to be mentioned because guest columns weren't rare. However, most people would put in a plug for the company they were associated with whereas Mr. Carson did not appear to do that.

MODEL "A"

Granby may have been doing well at this time but all was not well with many independent phonograph companies. A March announcement came that the A. J. Crafts. Co. from Richmond, VA had just filed for bankruptcy. Their liabilities were listed at $71,000 and assets were at just over $168,000. The company's *inability* to collect *outstanding* accounts was the reason for bankruptcy. In the age of in house credit, collecting accounts was key to success. This event only deserves mentioning to show the caliber of the Granby-Phillip Levy-American Home Furnishers. Corp. organization. Making money was not easy. Demand was not so high that it took no effort to be successful.

A smaller sized ad appeared in April edition of Talking Machine World and emphasized the fact that the Granby offered the dealer more than *three* times their percentage of profit with an investment of 30 per cent less when compared to other phonographs. The ad shows the Queen Anne console and the list price which was $300.00. At this point in April, ads still noted the Boston address for contact information.

What Is YOUR Percentage of Profit?

Queen Anne Console
Price $300

Suppose we could show you—and
PROVE—that

—with Granby you can make up to THREE TIMES
your *Present Percentage of Profit* at a Merchandise Investment up to 30 Per Cent less.

Would you be interested?

Why not ask us—Today—to prove it?

GRANBY PHONOGRAPH CORPORATION
General Sales Office
21 WEST STREET   BOSTON

Granby Sales Offices Move Back to Virginia

Big news came in May with the announcement that the sales offices were moved BACK TO NORFOLK from Boston. The announcement noted that the company had come to the conclusion (rather quickly....) that the sales offices should be in close proximity to production and headquarters. This particular announcement also stated that Edward F. Carson was coming back to Norfolk.

One could guess that the whole move to Boston was Mr. Carson's idea because as soon as the company made the announcement that the sales offices were coming back to Norfolk, Edward Carson resigned his position and took a job at another advertising agency. Mr. Carson had nothing but nice words to say about his time at Granby. He said that Granby had greater plans than

he was prepared to take on. He was off to pursue different things....
....*In the north*....

Granby Phonograph Corporation had indeed consolidated all of
its operations. It is during this time that all operations become
centered in Newport News, VA. The company, until then, operated
from Norfolk, VA with headquarters in the Levy Building on the
corner of Main and Church St. (which was also the HQ for all of the
Phillip Levy stores) Ads represented that the Norfolk, VA institution
simply had a factory in Newport News. But, from this point forward,
Granby Phonograph Corp. was completely a Newport News institution
with offices and factory advertised as being located in Newport News.
This is important to note in the Granby timeline. Ads that emphasized
"offices and factory in Newport News" appear after this time. *Of
course*, American Home Furnishers Corp. was still in charge.

Unique ad styles appear during this time period. A "Granby
Personal Message" appeared in Talking Machine World with a "letter
style" format that described the Granby and its good selling points.
The artistic period cabinets and the motor that was "built for Granby
by one of the biggest manufacturers in the country" were emphasized.
The dual tone arm that played both lateral and vertical 78 rpm records
and the concept that Granbys were "live merchandise" that would sell
were discussed in the ad.

Business was *indeed* doing well. A second "personal message"
style ad appeared in the July issue of Talking
Machine World and some impressive sales
statistics were revealed. During the period of May
25, 1921 to May 25, 1922, the store known as
Widener's, Inc. sold 1,003 Granbys. Mr. Speare,
manager of Widener's, Inc. noted that most of this
was due to word of mouth advertising. It seems as
though Granby owners were so happy with their
machines that they were quick to point out to their
friends and co-workers the machines nice features.

In summary, Mr. Speare said the Granby was selling itself. He also noted that the Model Number 13 Upright was especially popular. This phonograph was an upright in the Sheraton style and was moderate in price for the time, only $135.00.

July also brought the announcement of the enlargement of facilities in New York for Granby. Former distributor, M. M. Roemer was no longer affiliated with the company as a wholesaler and Granby took possession of its new enlarged quarters which was located at 37 W. Twentieth St. in rooms 904 and 905. One room provided excellent display and the other room was for storage. Warehouses were located on Sixteenth St. The increased facilities were obtained so Granby could better serve their dealers in the New York area. O. P. Graffen was in charge of the new offices.[31]

---

[31] "Granby Offices in New York." TMW. 6-15-1922. Page 180.

How Granby Viewed Itself In 1922

A unique ad appeared that gave insight into how the company viewed itself at this point in time. Granby described the time during and directly after World War 1 and related it to their business operations. They pointed out the fact that there were tons of companies making tons of phonographs because "people bought up everything." And then, competition began again and most of these companies failed because they did not have enough capital. Once these companies failed, the left over phonographs were "orphans" as Granby called them, without manufacturer backing.

The **first** fact that Granby stated in this ad was that "Granby Phonograph Corporation of Newport News, VA had a capital of 2.5 Million Dollars." The **second** fact was that Granby was "owned and financially backed by American Home Furnishers Corporation of Norfolk, VA, a concern that was capitalized at 4.5 Million Dollars." A later ad noted that they could afford to be liberal and that was the reason for their great deals. How's *that* for a marketing tactic? At this point in time the entire resources of American Home Furnishers Corp. was behind Granby that fact was the reason given for Granby's slow but steady growth. The ad finished by saying that "there is a generous offer awaiting you in Newport News." At this point in history, advertisements listed the capital of 2.5 million dollars just under their name in small font in their ads.

GRANBY Phonograph CORPORATION
Offices and Factory
Newport News,   Virginia

This text appeared at the bottom of Talking Machine World ads during this period.

In September, Mr. Thomas McCreedy was appointed as Sales Manager. Seen in this photograph from 1922, he brought a great deal of experience in the talking machine industry including his many acquaintances which made him very valuable as a sales manager in this field. He had knowledge of and had previous dealings with publishing homes and advertising agencies. This was a perfect match for his new duties with Granby. Mr. McCreedy made his office at the Granby HQ in Newport News, Va. Former Sales Manager, James F. Stapleton was given the title of Production Manager after the hire of Mr. McCreedy.

Like the previous year, a Granby Phonograph Exhibit was presented at the Ohio State Music Exposition on September 26th and 27th of 1922. Charles Kennedy, of the Kennedy-Schultz Co. who represented the Granby line in this area, and Thomas McCreedy, new Sales Manager, were in charge of the exhibit.[32]

New Discounted Prices

Mr. McCreedy was busy doing other things in addition to exhibits. The New York Evening Journal devoted 3 columns to Granby's advertising and progress. Granby's quality production, ample financial resources, and experienced men were featured. They made the announcement that advertising in the New York Journal and The American would begin for the fall. Ads presented a "comparative table" which showed previous prices and the new discounted prices of Granby phonographs. The ads also listed current dealers' names.

---

[32] "Granby Exhibit at Ohio Fair." TMW. 10-3-1922. Page 12.

The table below features the discounted prices offered on some, but not all, Granby models. Announcement was also made of the appointment of C. P. Chew as "special representative" of Granby during this time.

Model	Previous Price	New Discounted Price
Sheraton Upright	$140.00	$120.00
Early Virginian Upright	$200.00	$175.00
Louis XVI Upright	$275.00	$235.00
Early Virginian Console	$225.00	$175.00
Adam Console	$275.00	$200.00
Louis XVI Console	$325.00	$250.00
Queen Anne Console	$375.00	$250.00
Chippendale Console	$475.00	$325.00

The Granby Corporation Changes its Name

This is important in the Granby time line. A meeting of the board of directors was held on October 11, 1922 and it was resolved that the corporation would change its name from Granby Phonograph Corp. to Granby Manufacturing Corp. The name change was recorded on October 23rd. (If you own a Granby that says "made by Granby Mfg. Corp." it was made after this point in time.) But, why the name change? The 1923 ad in the city directory lists Granby as a maker of talking machines and *furniture*. Also, the initial charter of incorporation created and filed back in 1919 listed the purposes as "manufacturing furniture and fixtures of all kinds."

At this point in history, Granby felt the need to be portrayed as *more* than a phonograph company. And, market trends dictated that the corporation broaden its offerings in order to stay relevant and profitable. By 1922, Granby was also moving into bedroom furniture production. Interestingly, the $70,000 addition that fronted Virginia Ave. was largely to accommodate this new expanded product line. As a side note, other period publications from late 1922 and early 1923 specifically refer to the location as a furniture factory – *not* a phonograph factory.

A New Granby Phonograph Is Announced

Granby announced the addition of a new console to their model line in December. This phonograph was scaled down and called the "Apartment Baby Grand." This phonograph was created to meet the demand for a smaller console model and listed at $135.00.

Seen here, the phonograph was produced in Adam period design and had a tone modifier located inside the cabinet just behind the turntable. Other features included the same five ply panels used in full sized machines. The construction was guaranteed and it was offered in mahogany or walnut. Mr. Graffen, of the New York office, stated that demand for the instrument had already manifested before the phonograph was placed on the market. Although the factory addition was to accommodate the manufacture of the company's expansion into bedroom furniture, Mr. Graffen noted in Talking Machine World that construction of the new factory addition was being speeded up for the increased production of the *new phonograph* model. The first ad showcasing the new phonograph was also seen in the December issue of Talking Machine World.[33]

To summarize, by late 1922, the phonograph boom was reaching a point that only the best would survive. Granby felt the need to diversify by changing its name. And, we know now that the company was moving into other areas of furniture production. But, were phonographs *declining* in sales?

---

[33] December 15, 1922. Talking Machine World. Ad.

The Changing Phonograph Climate

On December 4th of 1922, some alarming data was released. The Department of Commerce had just released its figures comparing phonograph production of 1921 to that of 1919. And, on page 12 of the December 1922 edition of Talking Machine World, the figures were announced. Although we were now into 1922, the trend was concerning and worth mentioning at this point in the story. Total production of phonographs and related parts in 1919 amounted to a whopping figure of just over $158,000,000.00. In 1921, that figure had dropped to $98,164,000.00 which accounted for an estimated 38% decline. Employment was down during this period across the country and, specifically, wage earners in the talking machine industry had been decreased by 38%. All kinds of statistics were noted including needle production, cylinder phonograph and record production, and other products. Things were definitely changing and the numbers proved it! It is no wonder Granby was looking at expanding the product line at the factory to include household furniture. The trend appeared to show that phonograph production wasn't as lucrative as it once was. Harry Levy was already thinking ahead and diversifying the factory's product line…

Local Advertising in Newport News & Norfolk

Just like during 1921, while Granby was staying relevant on the national stage and trade journals, the advertising techniques used by the local stores back home in Virginia were not much different for 1922. The fancy ads with ornate illustrations of Granbys were still present, the basic format of the ads were unchanged. Like 1921, a Christmas Club was featured by Phillip Levy & Co. However, the Granby Christmas Club appears to be *anticipated* by customers in 1922. Phillip Levy advertised the club as "annual" and made references to the fact it is long awaited. However, the smaller vertical ads were not seen like the year before. Harry Levy still wrote his "letter" style ads. There is even one that recommended an Italian turkey stuffing recipe around Thanksgiving.

There seems to be some more local pride shown in 1922 when compared to previous years' ads. One ad that ran on November 29, 1922 tells that the Granby is *guaranteed* which is made possible "through our ownership and affiliation with the Granby factory. You will be supporting a home industry - that makes the phonograph worthy of a place in your home."

"The Granby phonograph is made in Newport News by expert craftsmen, who take pride in their work. This is an industry worthy of your support....." This ad tells a lot because Phillip Levy & Co. had not gone for the "local pride" aspect *at this level* before. It had been mentioned but not as a sales pitch.[34] However, it must have been nice to live in Newport News and buy a Granby that you know was made by your neighbors, just a short drive down the road. Many people passed the Granby factory on a daily basis, not too far from the shopping district on Washington Avenue where the Phillip Levy store was!

Choose the Granby by both your ear and your eye.

Hear The Granby Play Today And You'll Know Why People Who Own One, Tell Their Friends About It—

---

[34] November 29, 1922. Daily Press. Ad.

Typical ads noted the Granby phonograph was built to fit a price and it cost little or no more than a "cheap machine which was here today and gone tomorrow." The Granby was even offered on a free trial if the customer so desired. The Granby was still sold in weekly or monthly terms like years before. 5 double faced 10 inch records were included

The low and wide console cabinets were popular in 1922. Advertising that had previously listed 3 or 4 upright style phonographs now featured consoles. Granby still produced uprights but consoles were emphasized more in 1922.

Uprights had been on the market since around 1912 and they were looking a little outdated. 10 years later, the console was the "modern" instrument. Victor Victrola was also seen in console form at this time along with Sears, Roebuck's Silvertone phonographs, Brunswick phonographs and other makers. Keep in mind, uprights were still being produced and appreciated by the customer. It is just that the console was gaining popularity. Just as it is with consumer and buying trends today, when something is different, *it is new and exciting.*

By November of 1922, the Granby was being produced in 12 different period models according to local newspaper ads. That's 4 more than the original line of 8 back in 1920. There was initially a Sheraton upright in the original lineup that was later given the designation of No. 13, but now there were other models available in the Sheraton design along with Early Virginian models and the new Apartment Baby Grand that had recently been announced.

Phillip Levy & Co. ran an ad in The Virginian-Pilot on December 10, 1922 that was not seen in Newport News. In this ad, the *new* 1923 Granby phonographs were announced. However, pictured were the previously seen base models, Sheraton Console and Upright. The price was $125.00 for the console and $85.00 for the upright. The ad also made reference to Granby's success in other markets. It noted that "Granby distribution is not yet nationwide-but New York City's favorite instrument is the 1923 Granby!" The ad also stated that Granby sales currently led in Washington D.C. At this point in time, Granby was the phonograph of choice in New York City and Washington, D. C. The "southland's own phonograph" had made it.[35]

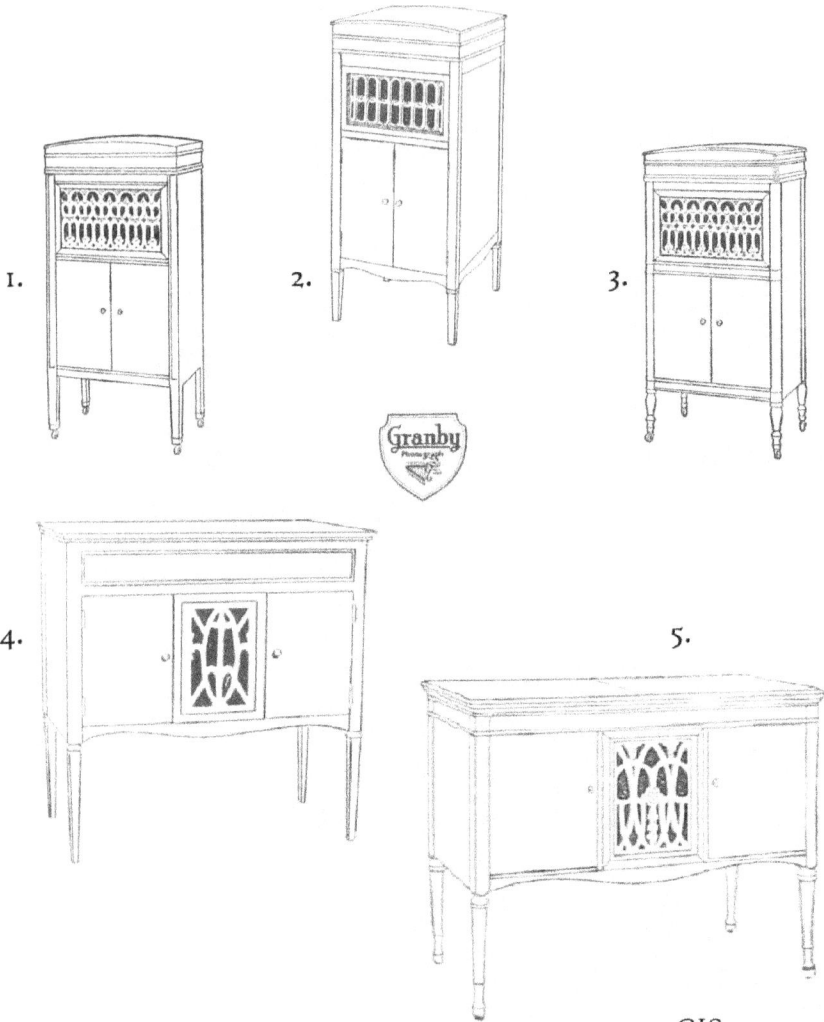

One – Sheraton No. 12, Two – Sheraton No. 10, Three – Early Virginian Upright
Four – Sheraton Console, Five – Early Virginian Console

---

[35] December 10, 1922. Virginian-Pilot. Ad.

PART V.

1923 ….and Beyond

Washington Avenue, Newport News

The Daily Press, October 15, 1949

Good Progress

The 1923 edition of the Newport News City Directory featured Granby's most impressive listing. Phonographs, talking machines, and furniture are listed as well as all of the officers with the corporation. Back on December 19th of 1922, a banquet was held at Guffanti's Restaurant in New York. All 12 of the New York employees of Granby were there. O. P. Graffen and C. P. Chew both made speeches at the dinner and discussed grand plans for 1923.[36]

Things were getting off to a good start. Already by February, the corporation reported good progress. According to Mr. Graffen, the first 2 weeks of February of 1923 were better than the whole month of January of the same year. Always the promoter, Mr. Graffen noted that January was "in itself a fair month."[37] Sales of the "new" Apartment Baby Grand of Adam design, introduced in late 1922, probably increased business. This was a time when Victor Talking Machine Co. had introduced its "Colony" model. Small consoles were in style. Mr. Graffen later noted that February sales were more than January and December and 10 times as much in February of 1922.[38] This was probably due to the major wholesale network that Granby had created since then.

On March 9, Granby made the announcement that possession of their new $70,000.00 addition to their plant in Newport News was near. Granby planned for expansion when the factory was designed back in 1920 and business was so well that the corporation was doubling the size of the plant in a wing that would front Virginia Ave. (now Warwick Blvd.) in Newport News. This addition completed the Granby factory and can be seen today in that form. Night work had to be undertaken by Granby to meet its demand before the completion of the new addition.

---

[36] "Banquet of Granby Forces." TMW. 12-15-22. Page 148.
[37] "Granby Sales Gain Steadily." TMW. 2-15-23. Page 142.
[38] "New York Granby Sales Grow." TMW. 3-15-23. Page 124.

A New Phonograph and Smaller Product Line

A new mini-console model was announced in April. Seen here, the Queen Anne console model number 215 cost $100.00 and, like the Adam design "Apartment Baby Grand," this model catered to the demand for smaller sized console models. A Granby advertisement noted that no machine, at double to price, had the appearance, plus the finish, plus the quality.[39] By May 1st of 1923, the corporation had placed on the market the last of its new five consoles. The model line then consisted of 5 consoles and 2 uprights that varied in price from $100.00 - $350.00.[40] It's pretty obvious that a *decrease* in the model line had occurred.

Mr. Oramel P. Graffen is the man who is in the public eye the most during 1923. Most announcements came from his New York wholesale branch and office for Granby. He was a hard worker and that worked to his disadvantage once when a Granby phonograph fell on his foot when he decided to help speed up deliveries in the shipping room. An article noted that this "inconvenienced him for some time." One can only imagine the damage a phonograph could do if it fell on your foot!

In June of 1923, Mr. Graffen visited the factory in Newport News and returned to New York very pleased with what he had seen. The new additions to the factory were done by this time but the company still found it necessary to work day and night in order to fill

---

[39] "Granby Console Is Popular." TMW. April 15, 1923. Page 176.
[40] "New Granby Models in Demand." TMW. April 15, 1923. Page 22.

orders for the "unprecedented demand." Mr. Graffen also announced that Mr. Louis Ziegler had been hired to work in the New York office as a "special sales representative." Mr. Ziegler was previously on the sales staff but did not go out and seek out new dealers. His new job as sales representative allowed him to do that. Like Mr. Graffen, he previously was employed by Columbia Graphophone Co. and on his first day out in the field for Granby, closed several new accounts.[41]

After some personnel changes that had occurred over the past few years, James Stapleton, seen here, was listed as the Manager of Granby Manufacturing Corporation in April of 1923. Advertisements from this time period only illustrate the *mini-consoles*; the Queen Anne console and the Baby Grand in Adam Design. However the complete Granby line was on display at the Grand Rapids Furniture Exhibition on July 1st. The phonographs were shown on the 9th floor of the Ringe Building. Grand Rapids was a well-known furniture city and the exhibition was well attended from people all over the country.[42]

The Exhibition in Grand Rapids would prove to be one of the last times the talking machine trade would here of Granby via Talking Machine World. Although 1923 brought general statements of success, no specific *new* dealers were ever named. However, business did appear to be booming although the model line was down to 7 with only 2 being stressed national advertising.

Interestingly, an article appeared a few months later regarding a new job that Mr. Graffen had taken but there was no mention of Granby. All advertisements abruptly stopped after July. It is certainly

---

[41] "Louis Ziegler with Granby Corp." TMW. June 15, 1923. Front page.
[42] "Granby Line at Furniture Show." TMW. July 15, 1923. Page 174.

an intriguing twist on a story that was as detailed (and fast) as the rise of Granby Phonograph Corp. Remember, this was the same company that seemingly came out of nowhere back in the Christmas season of 1919 with the Leviola. Ever since August of 1920, national attention was *truly* non-stop.

Meanwhile back home in Newport News, the fall of 1923 did not bring the advertising like what had been seen in 1921 and 1922 for the Granby. Actually, Phillip Levy & Co. wasn't advertising for phonographs *near* as much as they used to, even when compared to the days of Leviola and other phonographs. Stoves and furniture were emphasized in ads. *The Granby isn't even seen in most furniture ads.* The first ad that even mentioned the Granby phonograph appeared on December 9th. There appeared to be a Granby Christmas Club and there was a section that can be cut out and mailed in for information of Granby upright and console models. More ads for the Exchange Store's bargain phonographs are seen than anything. Harry Levy's "letter" style ad ran in mid-September and made a reference to the fact that the floors needed to be cleared and when that was done, the doors would close forever. American Home Furnishers had mastered the art of advertising and creating a sense of urgency. However, that was pretty intense language to use, to imply the doors would close forever... Below: The Daily Press, June 24, 1923, Newport News, Virginia

Phillip Levy & Co.
Going Out Of Business
IN
NEWPORT NEWS
Sale Now Going On

All "letter" style ads that had become a unique niche for Harry Levy, were after this point signed by Seymour Wyatt, the Newport News branch store's manager. His photo is seen on the left, taken in 1923. Only a few ads ran after Dec. 9th for the Granby. Familiar sales pitches like, "the Granby is being made today in our own factory" were seen. Phillip Levy & Co. delivered Granbys up until 12:00 am on Christmas Eve. The good old days of the fancy and elaborate Granby advertising were gone. There was something *different* about Phillip Levy & Co.

An ad that ran in October gave a little insight and stated that the store had its own wholesale division and central warehouse. $5,000,000 worth of business a year is done through a "command of the country's outlets." It was stated that the Phillip Levy store was part of a growing group of retail stores operating as one unit.

Of particular interest is an excerpt from a December 6, 1923 ad discussing the *reopening* of the Phillip Levy Exchange Store. This store had opened once before and was for inventory not quite up to the quality of Phillip Levy merchandise in the main store. Trade-ins and other bargain items were found at Phillip Levy's Exchange Store. "The new directing heads of the great Phillip Levy organization" were the ones that reopened the store. The Exchange Store is not the interesting concept here but the reference to the "new directing heads."

"Clearance Sale"   Main & Church Street, Norfolk, Virginia

Christopher James Stoessner Collection

Something Isn't Right

At this point in the story, it appears to be pretty obvious that something is brewing. But, American Home Furnishers Corporation was not a *small* company. They seemingly had risen to success. An informational and biographical publication put out in early 1923 offered a lot of insight. As stated, in April of 1923, American Home Furnishers Corporation owned and operated 18 retail stores, a furniture factory, and 22 warehouses that made up the wholesale division, serving over 1500 stores across the South. Totaled, the 22 warehouses held 1,134 train car loads of home furnishings. They stated that by now they had standardized all advertising and sales promotions and noted that the consolidation of the corporations had created a savings in the operations structure. The total volume of business in 1923 alone was projected to be over Six million dollars.

The corporation featured a central insurance department, traffic bureau, accounting department, new business bureau, and merchandise/advertising departments. These departments were centralized instead of having duplicate work performed at each branch location. Office managers received "class room training for establishing uniform methods" for handling records.

It was estimated that 600,000 customers entered the stores during a calendar year and between 45,000 to 55,000 of them had charge accounts. American Home Furnishers Corporation employed 800 people and operated a fleet of 43 delivery trucks and it took a total of 78 adding, bookkeeping machines, and typewriters to handle a days' business.

The Central Warehouse and Wholesale Division used this style of truck.

Christopher James Stoessner Collection

As speculated earlier, Granby confirmed by this point in history that their priority was furniture production – not necessarily *phonograph* production. Forty four-piece bedroom suits could be manufactured in one day, totaling 48,000 individual pieces a year. The recent addition of over 39,000 square feet helped to obtain these impressive production figures and the factory told that it was "oversold" 30 to 60 days in advance. The furniture was distributed all throughout the country, with an estimated 30% going to the Pacific coast.

The wholesale division featured 24 showrooms which accounted for over 10,000 square feet. A unique program was utilized in that a customer was allowed to enter these show rooms and select furniture. The selections where then charged to the retail store who had the account. This allowed smaller stores to direct their customers to the warehouse and not incur the overhead of stocking. A preplanned appointment time and card of introduction was utilized.

Harry Levy appeared to have done well following the tragic death of Phillip. He had surrounded himself with other prominent business men to help grow and advise him in his ventures. However, at the time these figures were being advertised to the public, all national advertising ceased in Talking Machine World.

A Newport News Factory Warehouse Circa 1923

Christopher James Stoessner Collection

Bankruptcy

One doesn't have to be a student of business or economic cycles to understand that sometimes, things go wrong. And, bigger is not always better when it comes to business operations. For example, there could exist a small group of 3 or 4 stores that are highly profitable and don't have very much in debt. Or, on the other hand, you could have a very large operation with multiple stores and a factory that carried too much debt. A simple downtown in the economy, a few slow months in sales, or accounts receivable that become difficult to collect can really damage an otherwise profitable business. Accounts Receivable is a great asset until it becomes uncollectable or *bad debt*.

The fact remained that on December 3, 1923; American Home Furnishers Corporation declared Bankruptcy and on January 26th of 1924, officially became the property of General Stores Corporation of Baltimore, MD. They delivered a certified check for the amount of $955,000 and assumed agreed upon liabilities according the newspaper accounts. With the liabilities, total consideration given was $1,387,000.00 with assets of the American Home Furnishers Corporation being quoted at over five million. The largest amount of money owed was to the Industrial Finance Corporation and this was *unsecured*. Arthur J. Morris was head of this organization which pledged its support and the merger had his blessing.

It is important to pause here and remember the merger that occurred a few years back with American Home Furnishers. Although consolidation helped *streamline* the operations, it had the potential to create a problem. For example, if one portion of the company encountered financial problems, the rest of the entity would inherit those problems. In hindsight, if the companies remained truly separate, maybe the stores could have been retained and manufacturing division sold off. Or, if the chain of retail stores would have remained at the original eight and not expanded, maybe profits could have been maintained. *History will never know.*

More details finally came out in the court case Levy vs. Industrial Finance Corporation argued on February 24, 1928 and decided on March 5, 1928. Court records show that Harry Levy and Esther Levy (Phillip's widow) owned 2/3 of the stock in American Home Furnishers Corporation. Mr. Levy received a 1.5 million dollar loan from Industrial Finance Corporation by overstating the assets of the corporation according to court records. The statement was "made in writing and known by him to be false."

In the beginning of 1924, General Stores Corporation was created to collect the assets and liabilities of the former American Home Furnishers Corporation which dissolved in 1923. Seen here, the brother to Harry Coplan and former Auditor and Secretary with the American Home Furnishers, Maxwell (M.L.) Coplan became Manager of General Stores Corporation. *The Granby corporation was no more.* Back on September 24, 1923, Landay Brothers announced in the Bridgeport Telegram that they had purchased the remaining stock of Granby Phonographs direct from the factory in Newport News. They offered the stock of 1,326 phonographs at half price. They noted that there were 16 period models to choose from and the Granby phonograph was well-known from *coast to coast.* The 1924 Newport News City Directory simply referred to the former phonograph factory as "Phillip Levy & Co. – Factory." On March 19, 1925, the deed was recorded; officially transferring the factory to General Stores Corp. and going forward, city directories would note this location as the "warehouse" for Phillip Levy & Co.[43] In 1927, Reliable Stores Corporation merged with General Stores Corporation who had acquired Phillip Levy & Co. and American

---

[43] March 20, 1925. Daily Press. Funiture Plant Deed Recorded.

Home Furnishers through bankruptcy. On May 2, 1938, L. U. Noland of Newport News announced that he would relocate his company to the former phonograph plant. He estimated the cost to remodel the plant at around $30,000.[44]

Granby Phonograph Corporation… or *Noland Green Apartments* as the property is currently known in 2018. The secret is out! Newport News was home to a talking machine factory and the building still stands.

Photograph by Christopher James Stoessner

---

[44] May 3, 1938. Daily Press. Noland to Expand Quarters and Move Firm Office.

Life After Granby

When I spoke with Harry Levy's daughter, Doris Reyner Levy Sostmann, she didn't recall the circumstances of why her father got out of the furniture business in Virginia. After making their home for many years at 918 Graydon Ave. in the Ghent section of Norfolk, she recalled the family moving to Hialeah, Florida in the mid 1920's. The appeal of Florida is understandable. In the 1920's ads were becoming very frequent for summer get-a-ways. Furniture stores often ran ads with bargain furniture that had been used the previous season in a "summer cottage." The economic boom of the 1920's was producing enough discretionary income to where Americans had second homes and vacation properties. It would seem completely logical that Harry Levy would see this market trend as a great opportunity.

Photograph: Upper Left, Harry Levy circa 1922

Men of the South: Courtesy of Sargeant Memorial Collection, Norfolk Public Library

Ms. Sostmann's recollections were correct. Research shows that Harry did indeed make his way to Florida and acquire the Seminole Bed Spring Manufacturing Co. He immediately expanded it to include a retail operation. He marketed this as a furniture store with "factory direct" savings. Many ads emphasized close out purchases from well-known furniture or mattress manufacturers. Modern day business enthusiasts will notice that factory direct and close-out furniture marketing is a concept still in use today. Note that Harry Levy utilized these techniques in the 1920's. Unfortunately, the Florida operation proved to be a short lived venture.

The factory was plagued by hurricane damage and a fire. By 1927, the family left Florida and made their way to Iowa for a brief period and then to Philadelphia. Always the family venture, Harry's half-sister, Julia Morris played a key role in business operations in Florida and Iowa before settling in Philadelphia and ultimately back in Florida. Ms. Morris lived to be 100 years old and died at her home in Deerfield Beach, Florida on July 3, 1998.

Harry Levy passed away on March 7, 1938 at the residence of his son, Milton Levy, in New York City. His death was the result of car accident he was in years before according to his daughter. He left his wife Celia; three daughters, Gertrude, Isabel, Doris; his son Milton; and three grandchildren, Joseph, Ann, and Charlotte. After spending his entire career in home furnishings, he was an Insurance Broker at the time of his passing and a resident of Washington DC.

A newspaper ad for Seminole Products in Florida which showcases Harry Levy's aggressive marketing style.

The Miami News, Wednesday, December 1, 1926

100,000 square feet of Factory Direct Savings

The Miami News, Sunday, December 6, 1925

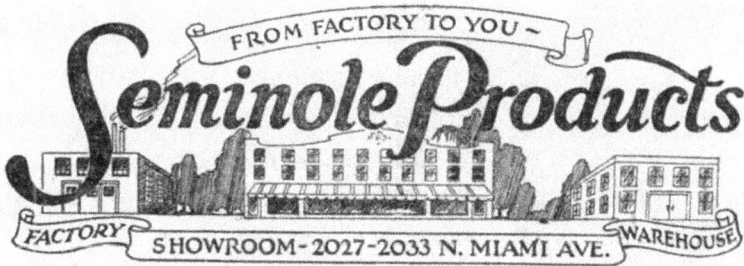

FROM FACTORY TO YOU ~

Seminole Products

FACTORY — SHOWROOM - 2027-2033 N. MIAMI AVE. — WAREHOUSE

To All **Virginians,** *in Miami and South Florida*

FOR the last thirty-one years I was a Virginian until I commenced manufacturing Seminole Products in Miami.

Not a day passes but some former customer stops me to say "hello." This happens everywhere I go; at my dentists, at my lawyers, at my tailors—and very often, when I go out to lunch. So I say—

"Thank You, **Virginians,** *for your warm welcome to me"*

A Message from Harry Levy

The Miami News, Sunday, July 12, 1925

111

Ms. Doris Levy Brenner Sostmann passed away after the interview for this research that was conducted back in 2003. She offered great insight into her life and it was a pleasure speaking with her and corresponding with her son, Mr. Joseph Brenner during the early stages of this project. Ms. Sostmann led a special life, as well, which included fond memories riding the handlebars of her chauffeur's bicycle to school when she was only 12. Among her many accomplishments, she founded Doris Brenner Interiors in Philadelphia and gained the respect of area painters, wallpapers, contractors, and upholsterers.

Percy Trilnick played a slightly smaller role than Harry Levy and other executives. His name appeared earlier in the story as a Manager of Phillip Levy & Co. in Newport News and periodically as a Salesman for Granby. His story is *quite* unique. A native of England, at age 22 in 1919, he had made his way to Newport News, VA. Later in life, he went on to create the Women's Fashion Export Group of Great Britain and is credited with popularizing American fashions in England through the use of fashion shows and importing. He was said to always be seen with a white carnation in the lapel button hole of his jacket. In 1941, Mr. Trilnick organized a large gathering at New York's Hotel Astor in which he was photographed with First Lady Eleanor Roosevelt. He passed away on October 18, 1956 in England. A young man in the home furnishings industry became a well-known name in the fashion industry.

Harry Coplan did not remain with the newly created General Stores Corporation like his brother, M. L. Coplan. They did both move to the Baltimore area but Harry had a successful career with Retail Stores Service Inc. where he was instrumental in business mergers. He passed away in January of 1974 in Baltimore. Harry is remembered by his grandson, Richard Coplan, as an ethical individual who always took the high road when dealing with high profile mergers.

This photograph contains four generations of the Coplan family. Harry Coplan is seated, his grandson Richard Coplan is standing on the left, and his son Asher Coplan is holding his great-grandson, Adam. (Richard's son) Circa 1972

Photograph Courtesy of Richard Coplan.

On an important side note, M. L. Coplan's son, Alfred became affiliated with Reliable Stores Corporation in 1950. Prior to that, he had the distinction of being the youngest person in Maryland to pass the exam to become a Certified Public Accountant in 1945, at age 20. Alfred became well-known in the Baltimore area and left quite a legacy in his own right due to his demeanor, charitable activities, and community involvement. Although the time period in this story did not *directly* reference him, I would be remiss to not mention his name and contributions. Mr. Coplan passed away in August of 2003.

The Sun, Sunday Morning, April 5, 1925

Baltimore, Maryland

Reliable Stores Corp.

Sinking Fund Gold 6's

Due October 1, 1937

The senior obligation of a Company operating
20 retail furniture stores in 14 large cities.
Net tangible assets $3,559 per $1000 Note.
1929 earnings over 6½ times interest charges.

Price 94 to net 7.05%

Descriptive circular on request

HORNBLOWER & WEEKS
ESTABLISHED 1888

BOSTON	Columbian Nat. Bank Bldg.	DETROIT
NEW YORK	Cor. Fourth Avenue	PROVIDENCE
CHICAGO	and Wood St.	PORTLAND, ME.
CLEVELAND	PITTSBURGH	PITTSBURGH
	Telephone Court 4010	

Members of the New York, Boston, Chicago, Cleveland, Pittsburgh,
and Detroit Stock Exchanges and the New York Curb Exchange.

Pittsburgh Post-Gazette, Thursday, March 27, 1930

Pittsburgh, Pennsylvania

Reliable Stores Corporation

This story would not be complete without touching on the
company that operated the Phillip Levy & Co. stores, as remembered
by most, from 1924 and onward. Baltimore native, Mr. Aaron Strauss
started his retail furniture store in Baltimore, MD with a capital of
$20,000.00 in 1892. Mr. Strauss expanded his stores slowly and
effectively. He established a location in Indianapolis, Indiana in 1898
and a location in Terre Haute in 1900. He was always "unhurried"
and seldom borrowed money from banks or individuals to finance his

acquisitions. For example, when buying a new business for expansion, he would negotiate a purchase price that amounted to around 10 to 15 percent and the balance would be made in 10 or so annual installments. He paid an estimated 75 cents on the dollar for accounts receivables and inventory. The profit margins of the store in the coming years would offset his installment payments and in some instances Mr. Strauss would come out ahead once the store was paid for. It makes total sense that his beginning capital of $20,000 in 1892 would increase and over 6,000,000.00 in 1925. *That is quite admirable.*

The furniture stores carried furniture from low to medium quality including floor coverings, refrigerators, washing machines, stoves, radios, china, as well as bicycles, baby carriages, and a line of toys during the Christmas season. It is interesting to note that just like the American Home Furnishers Corporation, Reliable Stores Corporation relied heavily on installment sales. As of 1937, over 95% of their business was installment sales. The company relied on "high markup on a slow turnover."

Stores affiliated with Mr. Strauss prior to the American Home Furnishers acquisition

Reliable Furniture & Carpet Co.	Indianapolis, Rochester, Detroit
Terre Haute Furniture And Carpet Co.	Terre Haute, Indiana
Hub Furniture Co.	Washington, D.C.
Christian Schmidt Furniture Co.	Newark, NJ
National Furniture Co.	Washington, D.C.
George B. Clark Co.	Bridgeport, Conn.
Julius Lindburgh Furniture Co. Inc.	Washington, D.C.
H. Crockin Furniture Co.	Norfolk, VA

Early on, the stores were operated as separate corporations in which Mr. Strauss oversaw. The headquarters was based at One South Howard St. in Baltimore. Mr. Israel B. Brodie provided a brief history of the corporation and was present and active in the American Home Furnishers Corporation acquisition. By 1924, Mr. Brodie, who had been legal counsel to Mr. Strauss since 1910, had earned his trust and developed a plan for the acquisition.

He proposed that Mr. Aaron Strauss be prepared to put a portion of his own money into the business and that he (Mr. Brodie) would take responsibility for any amount over said amount in order to make the purchase. His plan was structured so that the bankrupt properties could be brought up to a profitable status while operating as a *separate* unit from Reliable Stores Corporation. This would be a *trial* period. The name General Stores Corporation was chosen to absorb all of American Home Furnishers' properties. The proposal included the stipulation that *only* if General Stores Corp. became profitable would they then be absorbed into the Reliable Stores Corporation and, also, at that time the other stores that were working independently be merged, as well.

Mr. Strauss accepted Mr. Brodie's proposal. Mr. Brodie obtained loans in the amount of over $2,000,000.00 from New York and placed the bid in the United States District Court in Norfolk. They were the highest bid and were accepted. It was contested by creditors but ultimately worked out. The transition was not easy. General Stores Corporation was faced with a shortage of working capital during the period in which the reorganization occurred. It was an uneasy period but the merger ultimately worked out according to Mr. Brodie's plan. By 1927, the profitable General Stores Corporation was merged with Reliable Stores Corporation and they were off and running, with the Phillip Levy stores as a prominent division and big part of the success and branding.

Of particular interest to those interested in Norfolk, VA retail history, Reliable Stores Corp. also acquired the H. Crockin Furniture Company prior to the American Home Furnishers bankruptcy and merged the names of the two stores, creating *Crockin-Levy*. A meeting was held at 10:00 am on June 5, 1935 in Baltimore and the resolution was officially passed, creating a well-known furniture store name in the Norfolk area for years to come, see next page...

117

This photograph was taken around 1930, prior to the merger of the names. The building no longer featured the painted signage seen just a few years before.

Courtesy of Sargeant Memorial Collection, Norfolk Public Library

No story of retail enterprises would be complete without mentioning the stock market crash of October, 1929. As an example, Reliable's net sales in 1929 were over $13,000,000.00. In 1933, during the Great Depression, sales were less than $6,000,000. The International Statistics Bureau cited that retail furniture sales in 1932 were only 30% when compared to 1929. According to a report prepared in 1937, the company survived and found success due to sound policies, capable management, and "substantial goodwill." The company would also "eliminate unprofitable units" when necessary. (The general public would know this better today as "closing stores not making enough money.") Reliable branched out into the jewelry business in the 1930's acquiring locations in Texas and the S&N Katz Jewelry Co. of Baltimore, which included 14 locations. More furniture stores and jewelry stores were acquired over the next few decades due to Reliable Stores Corporation's "good locations, large buying power, and efficient personnel."

As a side note and *very* important fact, Mr. Aaron Strauss and his wife, Lillie created the Aaron and Lillie Strauss Foundation, Inc. in 1926, a charitable organization which continues to this day in the Baltimore area.

Reliable Stores retained the Phillip Levy name in Newport News and Richmond markets until April of 1987. At that time, the name was dropped and the stores were renamed Hub Furniture Centers. Prior to the name change, the stores were operated as many companies are today when a corporate entity chooses to retain the family name because of familiarity to the community.

One of the last Phillip Levy ads to be seen in the Virginia market

The Daily Press, April 10, 1987   Newport News, Virginia

119

On December 2, 1935, Phillip Levy & Co. took possession of this entire building located in the 2700 block of Washington Avenue under the direction of Reliable Stores Corporation. Mr. John J. Talman was Store Manager during this period.

The Phillip Levy & Co. name was carved directly into the surface of the black structural glass by Binswanger & Co. of Richmond. (12.1.1935 - Daily Press)

Photograph by Cheyne's Studio - Hampton, Virginia

Library of Virginia

120

Postlude

The story of the Leviola and the Granby Phonograph is a rather short one that spans from 1919 to 1924. But, this story is about much more than a phonograph. It is the story of the American dream that had roots back in the 1890's when the Levy brothers arrived in America and migrated to Norfolk, VA. For skeptics, it may be hard to imagine but this story proves that there was a time in our great country when immigrants could come here, start their enterprise, and watch it grow. A person did not need a rich financial backer or hidden secret. When Phillip Levy passed away in 1919, one newspaper account referred to him as "wealthy." Also, one can look at the legacy of Mr. Aaron Strauss of Baltimore and his Reliable Stores Corporation as a positive example of starting a business and seeing success. In the previous pages, this story is intertwined with family owned stores jumping on the bandwagon of the latest and most exciting item – it just happened to the phonograph in this time era. In the modern era, it has been the flat screen tv and then the latest and greatest cell phone. In the Levy's story, they were investing every ounce of their energy to provide for their family, make money, and leave their legacy.

What began as a simple quest for information about an antique phonograph opened the door to an amazing story that encompassed a chain of furniture stores and the tragedy of an entrepreneur taken before his time. His younger brother, probably heartbroken and in shock, stepped up and did the best he could. History shows us that Harry Levy apparently got caught up in the economic atmosphere and embraced rapid expansion instead of staying content. But, *can he really be faulted?* Phonographs were a profitable item in this time era. When Newport News branch store manager Harry Coplan presented his phonograph factory idea, Harry Levy approved it. And, for a time, the phonograph company flourished. Actually, they couldn't keep up with demand and immediately expanded the factory.

Always the forward thinker, when phonograph production showed signs of slowing in 1922, Harry Levy immediately expanded into bedroom furniture. Instead of sitting idle, upon the bankruptcy of American Home Furnishers' Corporation, he pursued opportunities in Florida, and then Iowa.

To summarize, Virginia and its early population centers including Norfolk, Newport News, and Richmond, is steeped in history that can be traced to the *founding* of the United States. There are several well documented histories of the areas' colonial roots, civil war history, and well-known business enterprises. There are numerous illustrations and books about those subjects well worth the time and read. But, from this day forward, let it be documented that Newport News, Virginia was famous for its talking machine known all over the nation in the early 1920's – the Granby Phonograph. Also, let history now remember the Levy family and their contribution to business and marketing concepts still in use to this very day. For a period in time, Phillip and Harry Levy were Norfolk's Greatest Home Furnishers. Shortly thereafter, the company, along with their factory in Newport News, became famous well outside of Norfolk.

The rear of Phillip Levy & Co.'s store on Broad Street in Richmond, Virginia

I took this photograph in August of 2004 and the lettering is still visible on the building in 2018

Christopher James Stoessner

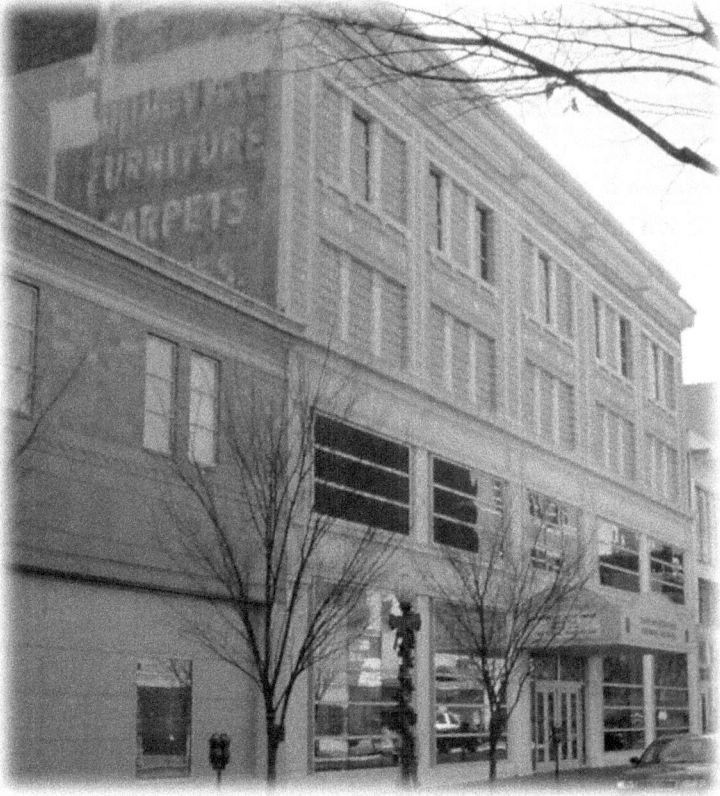

Phillip Levy & Co.'s former store on Granby Street in Norfolk, Virginia

Photograph taken in 2003 when the Phillip Levy & Co. sign was still visible

Following the death of Phillip Levy in 1919, Harry Levy made the decision to lease the building to Gilmer's, Inc. in order to receive some rental income that could be allocated to other ventures including the phonograph factory and growing chain of retail stores. When General Stores Corporation acquired the American Home Furnishers properties in 1924, this anchor location on Granby Street came with the deal. Gilmer's lease was not renewed. After interior alterations, the building began its new life as the Loew's State Theatre and opened to the public on Monday, May 10, 1926.

In May of 1910, scores of people visited the beautiful new furniture store operated by brothers, Phillip and Harry Levy. During the same month 16 years later, attendance records were broken in the same building but for a different purpose – a theatrical performance. Phillip Levy & Co.'s "Big Store" was ahead of its time in 1910 and one could even call it slightly "out of place." But, after 1926, the building would now go on to be etched in the memory of Norfolk and Hampton Roads locals as a theatre.

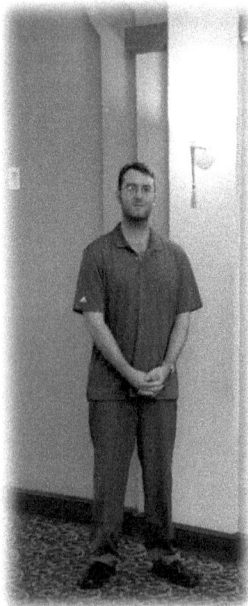

I had the opportunity to visit the TCC Jeanne and George Roper Performing Arts Center in February of 2018. This was a sentimental visit for me, as I had come to know the Levy family's story very intimately and to stand in their store was a special feeling. It was also a great opportunity to see a Norfolk cinematic landmark certainly special in its own right. It now serves as a state of the art performance venue and seats 900 guests. My thanks to Mr. Paul Lasakow for his time in showing me the venue.

Christopher James Stoessner, February 17, 2018

Part VI

A Reference Guide

A Sampling of Granby Phonograph Retailers

Phillip Levy & Co., Multiple Locations	Pollack's, Baltimore, MD
Exchange Furniture Co., Baltimore, MD	Harlow-Willcox & Co, Petersburg, VA
W. S. Arbaugh Furniture Co., Salem, OH	Widener's Inc., 14 Locations
C. H. Thuner Furn. & Carpet Co., St. Louis	Buettner Furniture Co, St. Louis, MS
Deeken Music Co., St. Louis	David's Furniture Co, St. Louis
George S. Hane, Philadelphia, PA	E. M. Hardesty Music Co, St. Louis
Howard and Winslow, Inc.	Hills, McLean, & Haskins, Binghamton, NY
J. E. and W. H. Nace, Hanover, PA	J. Johnson & Sons, Alliance, OH
Spear Music Co., Dover, OH	Leon Schoeppe, Philadelphia, PA
St. Louis House Furnishing Co.	S. Steinbrecher, Philadelphia, PA
L. M. Lytton, Burgettstown, PA	Tower Music Shoppe, St. Louis
Frey-Fisher Co., Cleveland, OH	Shipman Organ Co., High Point, NC
H. B. Bruck & Sons, Cleveland, OH	Ben W. Schwabacher, Lynch, KY
I. Namm and Son, Brooklyn, NY	Goosman Piano Co., Toledo, OH
Ludwig Baumann & Co., Newark, NJ	Federal Phonograph Co., Pittsburgh, PA
The Hecht Co., Washington DC	Landay Bros., Bridgeport, CT and others
Stix, Baer, & Fuller, St. Louis,	Gimbel Bros, Philadelphia, PA
M. Alpert and Sons, Scranton, PA	Smith Furniture Co, High Point, NC
Welborn Furniture Co, High Point, NC	S. Valente, Inc., Rochester, NY
Dyckman Grafonola Shop, NY	Walker Bros, Farnham, NY
Mitchell Furniture Co, Poughkeepsie, NY	Capital Talking Machine Shop, Brooklyn
D. R. Yarnell Music Store, Mansfield, OH	Erb's Music Ship, Hamilton, OH
AB Smith Piano Co, Akron, OH	Saul Birns, NY
Academy Phonograph Shop, NY	Harlem Music Shop, NY

Names to Know

Phillip Levy
Older brother of Harry, husband to Esther, founded Phillip Levy & Co. furniture stores, tragically killed in train accident in 1919; immigrated from Russia circa 1891 with Harry and sisters, Rosa, Mary, and Sophia; married Esther on 5:00 PM, 4.8.1897 at Cumberland St. Synagogue

Harry Levy
Younger brother to Phillip, husband to the former Celia Reyner, father to Milton, Doris, Isabel, Gertrude, co-founder of Phillip Levy & Co, inherited retail businesses after Phillip's death and founded phonograph manufacturing enterprise; immigrated with brother Phillip and sisters circa 1891 from Russia

Esther Levy
Wife of Phillip Levy, was officer and stock holder of Phillip Levy & Co. Inc. and American Home Furnishers Corp.

Celia Levy
Wife of Harry Levy, daughter of Joseph Reyner, sister of Harry Reyner of Newport News, mother to Milton, Doris, Isabel, and Gertrude; born in Maryland and parents were Austrian immigrants

Doris Reyner Levy Sostmann
Born Nov. 12, 1912, passed away on Dec. 11, 2006 in Philadelphia. Daughter of Harry Levy and interviewed by the author in 2003. Ms. Sostmann offered a great deal of insight into her (and her father's) life. It was a true pleasure corresponding with her and her son, Mr. Joseph Brenner.

Harry Reyner
Brother of Celia Levy, Vice President of Granby Manufacturing Corp., future city council member and Mayor of Newport News; key figure in contributions to Newport News and regional history

Harry Coplan
Originally affiliated with Phillip Levy & Co. Retail Store in Newport News, proposed phonograph factory concept to Harry Levy, originally a factory superintendent, became Field Sales Manager after Mr. Howard's resignation; moved to Baltimore after merger with General Stores Corp.; from Russia

Maxwell L. Coplan
Brother to Harry Coplan, father to Alfred Coplan. Auditor for American Home Furnishers Corp., affiliated with General Stores Corp. after merger where he served as Manager and Auditor; immigrated from Russia

Alfred I. Coplan
Son of M. L. Coplan, joined Reliable Stores Corp. as comptroller in 1950, became President and CEO in the 1980's, well known in business circles and for contributions to charitable and nonprofit causes in the Baltimore area

Tazewell Taylor	Secretary of Granby and Leviola Corporations, Board of Directors – American Home Furnishers Corp.
Edmond C. Howard	Director of Sales for Granby Phonograph Corp., pivotal in company's early growth and development in 1920 and 1921; patents filed during this time period for cabinet designs and unique features were submitted and signed by E. C. Howard
Edward Fraser Carson	Assistant General Manager of Granby Phonograph Corp., was hired after E. C. Howard resigned, ran advertising and sales departments; previously was General Sales & Advertising Manager of the White Hickory Motor Corporation, maker of White Hickory Trucks among other companies
Irving Beckhardt	Credit Manager, with American Home Furnishers Corp. from the beginning, affiliated with American Cabinet Mfg. Corp. where he purchased all of the raw materials
Crawford Theodore Westmoreland (C. T.)	Superintendent of Granby Phonograph factory, his name appears after Harry Coplan was acting as Field Sales Manager, designed some Granby cabinets and was respected for his wood working experience and knowledge
Charles F. Pitt	Vice President of American Cabinet Mfg. Corp when founded in 1919
Hugo H. Schumaker	Secretary and General Manager of American Home Furnishers Corp., associated with Granby and Phillip Levy & Co. for duration; city director of Norfolk shows him residing at the Monticello Hotel during this period
Arthur J. Morris	Founder of the Morris Plan for Industrial Banking, Vice President and General Counsel of Industrial Finance Corporation of New York, on Board of Directors for American Home Furnishers Corp. in 1923
Hugh M. Kerr	Board of Directors – American Home Furnishers Corp. in 1923, also President, Trust Company of Norfolk, VA
Harry C. Whiting	Manager of Granby Factory; listed as Office Manager in 1923 City Directory, resided in Buckroe Beach, VA
Benjamin Stafford	Superintendent of Granby Factory in 1923; born in Kernersville, NC on 05.26.1863, died 07.24.1944 in Newport News, VA; listed as a Cabinet Maker in city directories prior to his affiliation with Granby…and after.

James F. Stapleton   Sales Manager for Granby; listed as General Manager in 1923; formerly a Salesman with American Home Furnishers Corp.

Thomas McCreedy   Sales Manager for Granby, hired in September of 1922 following E. F. Carson's departure; formerly associated with Victor Talking Machine Co.

Oramel Peck Graffen (O.P.)   Manager of Granby Office and Warehouse in New York City, former salesman for Columbia Graphophone Co., born 05.29.1886

Louis Ziegler   New York Sales Representative, worked out of office operated by O. P. Graffen, went out into the field and obtained new dealers

Rene Maurice Jaccard   Final Inspector at Granby Factory; immigrated to America from Switzerland; was 25 years old in 1921, also resided in Ohio prior to Newport News, VA

Edward L. Ginsburg   Assistant General Manager for Granby and Factory Salesman

Percy Trilnick   Granby Salesman; began as a Salesman at Phillip Levy & Co. in Norfolk, promoted to management of store in Newport News with Mr. J. J. Talman in 1920, when 22 years old, born on 6.13.1897 in England, parents were both from Russia; died on 10.18.1956 in England; later in life was affiliated with the women's fashion industry in England

John J. Talman   Former Clerk with Phillip Levy & Co., was promoted to management of Newport News store when Harry Coplan began working with Granby factory full time in 1920; Born 12.01.1871 in Richmond, Virginia and died 10.09.1933

Carl Buechner   Granby Salesman

C. P. Chew   Special Sales Representative for Granby; hired in November of 1922, formerly with Brunswick-Balke-Collender Co.

Fred W. Connelly   NC Sales Representative, Covered High Point and all of North Carolina

R. R. Wilson   New York Sales Representative for Granby

Robert D. Duffy   Indiana/Central Kentucky Sales Representative for Granby. Worked out of Widener's location in Indianapolis.

Morris Fantile   Manager of Cincinnati Office for Granby; later noted as being associated with Widener's Grafonola Shop in November of 1922

Robert C. Clark Ohio/Eastern Kentucky Sales Representative for Granby. Worked out of Cincinnati.

S. Bemis Maine/New Hampshire Sales Representative for Granby

Austin L. Fordham Eastern PA Sales Representative for Granby after 12.01.1922

O. F. Jester Eastern PA Sales Representative for Granby

E. W. Schumaker St. Louis Area Factory Sales Representative for Granby

J. H. Stiff Southeastern Sales Representative for Granby; covered South Carolina, Florida, Georgia, Alabama, Tennessee, worked out of Atlanta, Georgia

F. Percy Loth On Board of Directors of American Home Furnishers in 1923, also President of W. J. Loth Stove Co. of Waynesboro, VA

W. A. Godwin President, Norfolk National Bank in 1923, originally a Vice President of Leviola Talking machine Sales Corp. back in 1919

M. M. Roemer Wholesale distributor for the New York area until June of 1921, office was located at 1123 Broadway

James G. Widener Owned 14 Widener's Inc. locations and struck a deal with Harry Levy to carry Granby Phonographs at all locations. 9 of the locations would serve as wholesaler distribution points

Charles H. Kennedy Partnered with Mr. Schultz; Granby Distributors based out of Cleveland, Ohio

H. C. Schultz Partnered with Charles Kennedy, see above

Lionel M. Cole Sales Manager of Iroquois Sales Corporation, a company pivotal in New York distribution in the early period

Fred Binger Sales Rep in Fort Wayne, Indiana, formerly associated with Columbia Graphophone Co.

AJ Heath President of A. J. Heath and Co. of Philadelphia, Granby distributor; also distributed Cirola phonograph

C. A. Malliet Vice President of A. J. Heath and Co., see above

A Complete Bibliography

I. **Books**

Newport News, Virginia, The Harbor of a Thousand Ships, 1921 Year Book. Printed by the Newport News Printing Co., Inc. Compiled by B. A. Ferry & Company, photographs by Holladay Studio

Men of the South, a Work for the Newspaper Reference Library. New Orleans, LA. Southern Biographical Association. 1922. Page 724. Compiled under the Direction of the James O Jones Co., New Orleans, LA.

Brown, Alexander Crosby. *Newport News' 325 Years, A Record of the Progress of a Virginia Community.* Published by the Newport News Golden Anniversary Corporation, October 13 – 18, 1946

Walker, Carroll. *Norfolk, A Pictorial History.* Virginia Beach, VA. Donning Co. Publishers. 1975

Haine, Edgar A. *Railroad Wrecks.* New York, NY. Cornwall Books. 1994

Hailey L. Fehner, and Schulwolf, Lisa P. *Celebrating the Past, Creating the Future, Improving Health Every Day.* Rockville, MD. Montrose Press. 2013. Copyright, Sentara Healthcare

Timothy C. Fabrizio, and Paul, George F. *Discovering Antique Phonographs 1877 – 1929.* Atglen, PA. Schiffer Publishing Ltd. 2000

Timothy C. Fabrizio, and Paul, George F. *The Talking Machine: An Illustrated Compendium 1877 – 1929.* Atglen, PA. Schiffer Publishing Ltd. 1997

Moody, John. *Moody's Analysis of Investments.* New York. Pages 1520-1521. 1921.

Banks, Benjamin A. *The Galaxy: A Magazine of Literature.* Norfolk, VA. Page 30. Volume One, Number Nine. May, 1908.

II.   **Web Resources and Online Articles**

Taylor, Todd. *Vinyl Audities, A Look at the History and Ideas that Keep Vinyl Records Spinning*
http://razorcake.org/vinyl-audities-a-look-at-the-history-and-ideas-that-keep-vinyl-records-spinning-by-todd-taylor/

Morris County Library. *Historic Prices in 1919.*
https://mclib.info/reference/local-history-genealogy/historic-prices/1919-2/

Furniture City History by the Grand Rapids Historical Commission. *Widdicomb Furniture Co.*
http://www.furniturecityhistory.org/company/3909/widdicomb-furniture-co

III.   **Interview(s)**

Sostmann, Doris Reyner Levy. Interview by Christopher J. Stoessner, April 2003. Tape Recording.

Coplan, Richard. Informal Discussion with Christopher J. Stoessner. October 2017.

IV.   **Legal Reference**

Appeal from Law and Chancery Court of City of Norfolk. *Phillip Levy & Co. v. Davis.* Jan. 15, 1914.

U.S. Supreme Court. *Levy v. Industrial Finance Corporation, 276 U.S. 281 (1928). Levy v. Industrial Finance Corporation et al. No. 217.* Argued February 24 1928, Decided March 5, 1928

V.   **Interment Records: Forest Lawn Cemetery, City of Norfolk, VA**

Levy, Esther	March 1, 1953
Levy, Harry	March 9, 1938
Levy, Phillip	January 16, 1919
Levy, Celia Reyner	January 9, 1980

VI.   Newspaper Advertising

See Attached Spreadsheet. Numerous advertisements from the time
period of 1919 – 1925 were observed and documented via Microfilm
and Online. In the case that ads were repeated/duplicated during
multiple editions, only one date is entered for reference. Illustrations in
the text are cited directly below the inserted photograph.

MN	DY	YR	Name of Publication	City	Article Title or Ad Summary
4	8	18 97	Norfolk Virginian	Norfolk	Phillip/Esther Levy Wedding Announcement
12	30	19 00	Virginian-Pilot	Norfolk	Horse became Unmanageable
3	20	19 06	Daily Press	Newport News	Harry/Celia Levy Wedding Announcement
1	13	19	Virginia-Pilot	Norfolk	21 Killed & 3 Injured Near Batavia
1	14	19	Virginia-Pilot	Norfolk	Phillip Levy is Killed in Wreck on NY Central
1	14	19	Daily Press	Newport News	Philip Levy Killed in NY Central Wreck….
1	16	19	Daily Press	Newport News	Body of Phillip Levy Identified
7	29	19	Daily Press	Newport News	Phonographs to be Manufactured
9	5	19	Daily Press	Newport News	Phonograph Plant Now in Operation
9	10	19	Daily Press	Newport News	Deadlock Broken in Paving Scheme After Argument
9	22	19	The Sheboygan Press	Wisconsin	Early Crystola Ad
11	16	19	Daily Press	Newport News	Large Leviola Ad: 200 Machines, First Come…
11	21	19	Daily Press	Newport News	Ad: 43 Leviolas sold in First 2 Days of Sale….
11	22	19	Daily Press	Newport News	Leviola Photo In Ad with Trademark Logo
12	7	19	Daily Press	Newport News	American Cabinet Company Builds New Factory Here
12	14	19	Daily Press	Newport News	A Solid Trainload of Leviolas
1	13	20	Daily Press	Newport news	Phillip Levy History Ad

MN	DY	YR	Name of Publication	City	Article Title or Ad Summary
5	2	20	Daily Press	Newport News	American Cabinet Plant Large One
5	23	20	Daily Press	Newport News	Granby Ad: Models A, B, and C explained and illustrated
7	17	20	Richmond Times Disp.	Richmond	American Home Merger Advertisement
7	26	20	Richmond Times Disp.	Richmond	Parachute Jumper and Airplane Stunts
9	1	20	Daily Press	Newport News	150 Phonographs at Big Reductions
9	3	20	Daily Press	Newport News	High Grade Phonograph Sale
10	27	20	Daily Press	Newport News	Model C: Mahogany, Oak, Burled Walnut $115
11	6	20	Virginian-Pilot	Norfolk	$1.00 Delivers this Handsome Phonograph
11	8	20	Daily Press	Newport News	Machines Slightly Used for Demonstration...
11	10	20	Daily Press	Newport News	Model B: $2.00 per Week
11	10	20	Virginian-Pilot	Norfolk	$1.00 admits, Xmas Club, Unknown Pictured
11	11	20	Daily Press	Newport News	Columbia Grafonola Ad
11	14	20	Daily Press	Newport News	Place Your Order at Once
11	21	20	Daily Press	Newport News	$1 Delivers This Granby: Store Open til 10 PM
11	21	20	Daily Press	Newport News	Model B: Mahogany, Oak, Burled Walnut $135
11	23	20	Daily Press	Newport News	Join our Xmas Club: Model C Pictured
11	30	20	Daily Press	Newport News	$1 down delivers Granby
12	2	20	Daily Press	Newport News	Model B: Join Our Christmas Club
12	3	20	Daily Press	Newport News	$2 delivers Granby: Model B Pictured
12	7	20	Daily Press	Newport News	$2 Per Week, Model B: $25 worth of Rec. Free
12	10	20	Daily Press	Newport News	Granby Phonos at Half Price: NN Phono Supp.

MN	DY	YR	Name of Publication	City	Article Title or Ad Summary
12	12	20	Daily Press	Newport News	$2 delivers Granby: 25 packages/needles Free
12	14	20	Daily Press	Newport News	Model B: $10 worth of Records Free
12	16	20	Daily Press	Newport News	Fergusson's Victrola Ad
3	27	21	New York Times	New York	Roemer Ad showing Lineup of 8
9	24	21	Daily Press	Newport News	After Supper…. What Then?
10	23	21	Daily Press	Newport News	Granby Centered in Furniture Ad
10	25	21	Daily Press	Newport News	Small Ad: Easy Terms, Plays all Records
11	9	21	Daily Press	Newport News	Ad Showing Queen Anne Console
11	9	21	Daily Press	Newport News	Ad: Breakdown of Christmas Club Payments
11	14	21	Daily Press	Newport News	Happy is the Housewife: works to Granby…
11	22	21	The Salem News	Salem, OH	Ad: Virginia Granby will Appear
11	23	21	Virginia-Pilot	Norfolk	$5 Sends You This Beautiful Granby Phono…
11	24	21	Daily Press	Newport News	Granby: What it Means to Children
12	4	21	Daily Press	Newport News	Phillip Levy's Christmas Lamp Club
12	16	21	Daily Press	Newport News	Letter Ad: Making It Easy to give a Phono.
12	20	21	Daily Press	Newport News	Showing Uprights, Lasting Gift, etc.
11	19	22	Daily Press	Newport News	Granby Plant Here is Building Big Addition: Will Increase Output
11	26	22	Daily Press	Newport News	Choose Granby by Ear and Eye
11	29	22	Daily Press	Newport News	12 Period Models, in Our Own Factory
12	10	22	Virginia-Pilot	Norfolk	New '23 Sheraton Upright & Console
12	12	22	Virginia-Pilot	Norfolk	The New '23 Upright Sheraton

MN	DY	YR	Name of Publication	City	Article Title or Ad Summary
12	19	22	Roanoke World News	Roanoke	Christmas Granby Offer (12 Models)
9	4	23	Bridgeport Telegram	Conn.	Landay Bros. Buyout of All Granby Phono.
12	9	23	Daily Press	Newport News	Granby in Furniture Ad: Rare in '23
1	28	24	The Bee	Danville, VA	General Shake Up: Property of Gen. Stores....
1	30	24	The Bee	Danville, VA	Sale is Confirmed (to General Stores)
5	16	24	Daily Press	Newport News	Rountree-Tennis Brunswick Ad
3	20	25	Daily Press	Newport News	Furniture Plant Deed Recorded
6	29	25	Miami Daily News	Miami	Furniture Firm will Conduct Hialeah Plant
7	12	25	Miami Daily News	Miami	Harry Levy Introduction Ad
3	11	26	Daily Press	Newport News	Console Phonograph Not Named Granby
8	16	26	Miami Daily News	Miami	Seminole Co. Blaze
12	1	26	Miami Daily News	Miami	Seminole Co. Sale Ad w/ H. Levy
3	8	38	Daily Press	Newport News	Harry Levy Dies at Home of Son
5	3	38	Daily Press	Newport News	Noland to Expand Headquarters
1	8	1980	Daily Press	Newport News	Celia Reyner Obituary
3	25	87	Daily Press	Newport News	Phillip Levy to Change Name
7	5	98	Daily Press	Newport News	Julia Morris Obituary
8	22	2003	Baltimore Sun	Baltimore, MD	Alfred I. Coplan Obit/Biography

VII.   Trade Journals   See Associated Spreadsheet

Numerous articles are cited as first hand documentation for this research. The periods observed were from 1919 to 1924. These records were made available via Interlibrary loan and viewed on Microfilm during 2002 – 2004. Figures, quotes, names, and industry statistics are referenced accurately.

The Talking Machine World					
Edward Lyman Bill Inc., 373 Fourth Ave., New York (Monthly)					
Advertisement of Article Title	PAGE	MON	YR	VOL	#
Demand for Better Furniture Stimulated by Artistic.... T. M. Cabinets	56	4	20	XVI	4
Ad: A. J. Crafts Piano Co.	188	7	20	XVI	7
Ad: United Phonograph Motors	219	7	20	XVI	7
Granby Phonograph Corp. Now Making Deliveries	56	8	20	XVI	8
Ad: Four Page Ad from Pages 100 - 104 Introducing Lineup	100	8	20	XVI	8
Ad: Lampograph	not given	8	20	XVI	8
Ad: Meisselbach Motors	not given	8	20	XVI	8
Rotarians Guests of Granby Co. (Harry Levy Gives Tour Aug. 3)	208	8	20	XVI	8
An Interesting Publication (catalog showing eight models)	67	9	20	XVI	9
Ad: Double Page Ad from Pages 100 - 101 showing models	100	9	20	XVI	9
Pays Tribute to Trade Paper	203	9	20	XVI	9
Granby Distributors Appointed	104	10	20	XVI	10
R. J. Waters Has Granby Representation (Chicago)	143	10	20	XVI	10
Grand Rapids a Great Talking Machine Center	178	10	20	XVI	10
Granby Jobbers in New York (Ziegler, Baker, and Johnson)	207	10	20	XVI	10
Ad: What the Granby Selling Franchise Really Means	72	11	20	XVI	11
E. C. Howard Westward Bound	79	11	20	XVI	11

Advertisement or Article Title	PAGE	MON	YR	VOL	#
Latest Granby Literature	97	11	20	XVI	11
Granby with A. J. Heath and Co.	113	11	20	XVI	11
Clever New House Organ Issued: "Melodie" Announced	136	11	20	XVI	11
Rotogravure Mailing Cards	35	12	20	XVI	12
Ad: We Will Help You Sell the Granby (Adam Upright Pictured)	72	12	20	XVI	12
An Attractive Granby Slogan	79	12	20	XVI	12
Ad: Iroquois Sales Corporation Announcing Affiliation	80	12	20	XVI	12
Why Optimism Should Prevail: M.M. Roemer Takes on Granby	180	12	20	XVI	12
Adopt a Very Clever Trade-Mark	185	12	20	XVI	12
Ad: Granby Phonographs are Selling Despite So Called Depression	32	1	21	XVII	1
An Enviable Sales Record: Sell $67,000 Worth of Machines	55	1	21	XVII	1
Ad: An Interesting Fact - With a Moral	32	2	21	XVII	2
Granby Manager in New York	91	2	21	XVII	2
Closes Many Accounts	158	3	21	XVII	3
Ad: Beating the Tom Tom	28	4	21	XVII	4
Granby Campaign in New York	62	4	21	XVII	4
Dinner Given to Granby Force (at Hotel Warwick)	77	4	21	XVII	4
Granby Display at Adelphia Hotel	103	4	21	XVII	4
Increases Its Sales Force	165	4	21	XVII	4
Organize United Phonograph Dealers Association	39	4	21	XVII	4
To Feature the Granby Line (Federal Phonograph Co.)	51	4	21	XVII	4
Granby Dealers Meeting with Success	84	4	21	XVII	4
Occupies New Quarters	21	5	21	XVII	5
Ad: A Message of Much Meaning to Every Dealer	28	5	21	XVII	5
Granby Phonograph in India	55	5	21	XVII	5
Two New Retail Concerns	59	5	21	XVII	5
Looking for Big 5 Business (E. B. Shiddell Co.)	84	5	21	XVII	5
A. J. Heath & Co. Report Progress	95	5	21	XVII	5

Advertisement or Article Title	PAGE	MON	YR	VOL	#
Ad: Is Your Business Insured	12	6	21	XVII	6
Granby Line in Widener's Stores	50	6	21	XVII	6
L. M. Cole Back at his Desk	66	6	21	XVII	6
No Longer with the Company (6 6: MM Roemer no longer)	124	6	21	XVII	6
R. R. Wilson to represent Granby (in New York)	165	6	21	XVII	6
Ad: Why did Widener Do It?	20	7	21	XVII	7
Co-operating with Granby Trade	24	7	21	XVII	7
Granby Line Going Well at Widener's	69	7	21	XVII	7
Granby Jobbers in Indianapolis (Robert D. Duffy salesman)	82	7	21	XVII	7
New Cleveland Concern to Distribute the Granby	126	7	21	XVII	7
Take on Granby Agency	139	7	21	XVII	7
Receives Line of Granby Machines	158	7	21	XVII	7
New Buildings for Granby Corp.	177	7	21	XVII	7
Wanted Ad: Salesman for Granby	179	7	21	XVII	7
Ad: After You Buy Phonographs, You Want to Sell Them	20	8	21	XVII	8
Beckhardt New Credit Manager	26	8	21	XVII	8
E. F. Carson is General Manager	43	8	21	XVII	8
To Locate in Philadelphia	136	8	21	XVII	8
Had Interesting Experiences	143	8	21	XVII	8
Howard Resigns from Granby Co.	21	9	21	XVII	9
New Sign on Granby Factory	21	9	21	XVII	9
Granby Works With You and For You	33	9	21	XVII	9
A Real Fountain of Knowledge: C. T. Westmoreland	42	9	21	XVII	9
Delegates Visit Granby Factory	45	9	21	XVII	9
Beckhardt Undergoes Operation	49	9	21	XVII	9
Inaugurates Fall Campaign	59	9	21	XVII	9
To Represent the Granby: A. B. Smith of Carnegie, PA	80	9	21	XVII	9
Dealers who have taken on the Granby	94	9	21	XVII	9
Granby at Children's Picnic	96	9	21	XVII	9
When Figures Count	134	9	21	XVII	9

Advertisement or Article Title	PAGE	MON	YR	VOL	#
New Granby Agency in Alliance (J. Johnson Parade)	6	10	21	XVII	10
Ad: The Time Is Ripe (Louis XVI Console)	14	10	21	XVII	10
Extends Activities in the South	19	10	21	XVII	10
New Granby Dealers in St. Louis	31	10	21	XVII	10
O. P. Graffen with Granby Corp.	37	10	21	XVII	10
Granby at the Ohio Convention	42	10	21	XVII	10
Display at Illonois State Fair	62	10	21	XVII	10
Increase in Volume of Sales	102	10	21	XVII	10
Elaborate Opening in Alliance, Ohio (parade pic)	106	10	21	XVII	10
Hard Work Gets Business	142	10	21	XVII	10
New Granby Models Announced (Beckhardt Kiwanis Tour)	86	10	21	XVII	10
Ad: Promise and Performance	24	11	21	XVII	11
Kennedy-Schultz Co. Developments (Invitations)	90	11	21	XVII	11
Opens Sales & Display Rooms (A. B. Smith Pittsburgh)	107	11	21	XVII	11
Iowa Columbia Sales Force	149	11	21	XVII	11
Granby Campaign in St. Louis	32	11	21	XVII	11
J. G. Widener Visits Branch Stores	86	11	21	XVII	11
Two Join Widener's Staff	102	11	21	XVII	11
E. C. Howard in Oakland (wife and daughter Janet)	134	11	21	XVII	11
A Busy Granby Factory (overtime)	170	11	21	XVII	11
Ad: What is there in it for me? Queen Anne Upright Pictured	28	12	21	XVII	12
Exhibit that Attracts Attention (Hight Point Furniture 12 4)	40	12	21	XVII	12
Kennedy-Schultz's Granby Drive (Miss Granby's Identity?)	132	12	21	XVII	12
Make Shipment to India	144	12	21	XVII	12
Granby Activities in St. Louis	160	12	21	XVII	12
Granby Quaker City Dealer	22	12	21	XVII	12
Speare Co.'s Artistic Publicity	84	12	21	XVII	12
Goes After Trade and Gets It	3	1	22	XVIII	1
New Granby Distributors	10	1	22	XVIII	1
Ad: showing Granby Models	28	1	22	XVIII	1

Advertisement or Article Title	PAGE	MON	YR	VOL	#
Paul Zerrahn with Widnener	68	1	22	XVIII	1
Improving Conditions Help Business in St. Louis	85	1	22	XVIII	1
Granby Signs on Door Knobs	78	1	22	XVIII	1
Ad: Granby works with you and for you: Louis XVI console pictured	44	2	22	XVIII	2
Granby Grows in Popularity	56	2	22	XVIII	2
Granby Sales Offices in Boston	72	2	22	XVIII	2
Plan two new Granby Warehouses	145	2	22	XVIII	2
Brain Work in Salesmanship a Decided Essential	48	3	22	XVIII	3
The Progress of the Granby	126	3	22	XVIII	3
Ad: What is your percentage of profit? QAC pictured	78	4	22	XVIII	4
Granby Offices Now in Norfolk	14	5	22	XVIII	5
Ad: What is your percentage of profit? QAC pictured	39	5	22	XVIII	5
Kennedy-Schultz Co. Reorganization	77	5	22	XVIII	5
Edward F. Carson's New Post (resignation from Granby)	112	5	22	XVIII	5
Schwabacher adds Okeh Records	18	6	22	XVIII	6
Granby Personal Message Number Two	22	6	22	XVIII	6
H. B. Bruck and Sons in New Location	148	6	22	XVIII	6
Granby Offices in New York	180	6	22	XVIII	6
Ad: Widener sells 1,003 Granbys: No. 13 Upright Pictured	22	7	22	XVIII	7
Ad: Are you selling Orphan Machines? EVC No. 51 Pictured	22	8	22	XVIII	8
Appointed Granby Sales Manager: Thomas McCreedy Pic	3	9	22	XVIII	9
Ad: Is there a Mystery in Your Mind?	14	9	22	XVIII	9
Granby Exhibit at Ohio Fair, October 3	12	10	22	XVIII	10
Ad: No Better Talking Machine than Granby Can Be Made	144	10	22	XVIII	10
Great Granby Fall Campaign	50	11	22	XVIII	11
Fred Binger with Granby	141	11	22	XVIII	11
Dealers Encouraged Over Outlook	154	11	22	XVIII	11
Ad: List Prices Reduced: Sheraton Console 250 Pictured	164	11	22	XVIII	11

Advertisement or Article Title	PAGE	MON	YR	VOL	#
Decrease in Talking Machine Field	12	12	22	XVIII	12
Granby Corp. Changes Name	12	12	22	XVIII	12
Working for Christmas Sales	82	12	22	XVIII	12
Ad: Granby Responds to the Demand: Granby Short Adam Console	155	12	22	XVIII	12
An Attractive Granby Souviner	98	12	22	XVIII	12
November Totals Reach High Mark	131	12	22	XVIII	12
Banquet of Granby Forces	148	1	23	XIX	1
Ad: Big Liberal Discounts	45	1	23	XIX	1
Ad: The Apartment Baby Grand of Phonographs	10	2	23	XIX	2
Granby Sales Gain Steadily	142	2	23	XIX	2
Ad: The Apartment Baby Grand of Phonographs (Adam)	31	3	23	XIX	3
New Granby Plant Soon Ready (street level pic of const.)	117	3	23	XIX	3
New York Granby Sales Grow	124	3	23	XIX	3
New Granby Models in Demand (stating 7 con. And 2 uprights total)	22	4	23	XIX	4
Desk Clock for Granby Dealers	174	4	23	XIX	4
Granby Console is Popular (first time QAC mini is seen)	176	4	23	XIX	4
McCreedy Joins Strong Record Co.	3	5	23	XIX	5
Ad: The Greatest Value: QAC 215 MINI shown only	72	5	23	XIX	5
Granby Popularity Growing	168	5	23	XIX	5
Louis Ziegler with Granby Corp.	3	6	23	XIX	6
New Store in Kingston, NY	51	6	23	XIX	6
Ad: A Combination that Can't Be Beat: Adam and QAC 216 Pictured	61	6	23	XIX	6
Recovering From Accident (O. P. Graffen)	178	6	23	XIX	6
Granby Line at Furniture Show	20	7	23	XIX	7
Ad: A Combination that Can't Be Beat: Adam and QAC 216 Pictured	38	7	23	XIX	7
O. P. Graffen's Important Position (new job with Vox Corp.)	94	11	23	XIX	11

Presto: The American Music Trade Weekly					
Presto Publishing Co., 407 Dearborn St., Chicago, Illonois,					
	PAGE	MON.	YR	EDIT.	
Talking Machine Notes (building of Leviola factory)	25	1	20	1745	
Active Newport News Plant	26	4	20	1761	
Busy in Newport News	25	5	20	1766	

VIII.   Corporate Records

Certificate of Incorporation of Leviola Taking Machine Sales Corporation
August 26, 1919

Certificate for Amendment to the Charter of the Leviola Talking Machine Sales
Corporation   February 16, 1920

Amendment: Granby *Phonograph* Corp. to Granby *Manufacturing* Corp.
October 23, 1922

Certificate of Amendment to the Charter of Granby Manufacturing Corp.
February 15, 1926

Certificate of Incorporation of American Home Funishers Corporation
April 22, 1916

Certificate of Incorporation of American Cabinet Manufacturing Corporation
April 16, 1919

Agreement of Merger & Consolidation: American Cabinet Manufacturing
Corporation, American Home Furnishers Corporation, and Phillip Levy & Co.,
Incorporated under the name: American Home Furnishers Corporation
July 27, 1920

Certificate for Reduction of Capital Stock of American Home Furnishers Corp.
Sept. 20, 1922

Creation Document: Phillip Levy and Company, Incorporated
February 15, 1919

Certificate of Incorporation of Phillip Levy & Company, Incorporated
January 4, 1924

Documentation of Certificate of Incorporation of Reliable Stores Corporation
     May 11, 1925

Meeting Minutes: Combining names of two furniture stores into one; Crockin-Levy Company, June 5, 1935

Meeting Minutes: Regarding Esther Levy (widow of Phillip Levy) to remain as Agent of Reliable Stores Corporation and her salary (amount withheld by author)
     April 25, 1932

American Home: A Story In Pictures of the Plans, Properties, and Operations of the American Home Furnishers Corporation.
     (Christopher J. Stoessner Private Collection)

Brodie, Israel B. The Story of Reliable Stores Corporation. Not published. personal account prepared for Board of Directors and Officers of the Company. Circa 1962.
     (Christopher J. Stoessner Private Collection)

Examination of Reliable Stores Corporation and its Subsidiaries. Not published. March 31, 1937

> *"I have chosen to withhold any and all sensitive financial or personal information. The only figures included in this written history are figures that relate to the trends in the home furnishings businesses and/or figures made available to the **public** at various times through publications, stock offerings, or public notices. In some cases, figures were rounded off or omitted, out of respect to the individuals involved in these enterprises."*

Christopher J. Stoessner

IX.   City Directories

Several city directories in Virginia, Florida, and others were briefly consulted to observe store openings, closings, family migrations, etc. Those specifically referenced in this history are listed below:

Hill Directory Co. Inc. *Norfolk and Portsmouth City Directory 1920-21.* Page 593. 1921

Newport News City Directories. *1919 – 1926.* Consulted for listings concerning the factory, retail operations, persons affiliated with the companies, and company name changes. These records were observed by the author at the Main Street Library, 110 Main Street, Newport News, VA 23601 in the *Virginiana Room.*

Baltimore City Directory. Page 505. 1928

X.   **Armed Services Registration Card(s)**

Harry Coplan. June 5, 1917 (WWI) and April 25, 1942 (WWII)

XI.   **Federal Census Records**

The records were consulted for documenting the location, family members, job titles, for key individuals and their family members;
Years: 1900, 1910, 1920, 1930

XII.   **Marriage Records**

Rene Jaccard and Helen Sacstroh. Hamilton, Ohio. June 20, 1923.

Phillip Levy and Esther Levy. Norfolk, VA. April 8, 1897.

Harry Levy and Celia Reyner. Newport News, VA. April 3, 1906.

XIII. **Death Certificates**

Phillip Levy. State of New York Department of Health. January 12, 1919.

Harry Levy. Department of Health of the City of New York. March 7, 1938. Reg. #5336

XIV.   **Birth Certificates**

Doris Levy. Certificate of Birth: Commonwealth of Virginia. Nov. 12, 1912.

Christopher James Stoessner

pronounced stess – ner, silent "o"

Born in Newport News, Virginia, Chris lived in the Denbigh area before his family relocated to Smithfield, Virginia in the late 1990's. He graduated from Smithfield High School in 2001. During his teenage years, he developed an interest in history and antiques and by age 14, was buying and selling antiques as a hobby. At age 17, he started his own antiques business located at 119 N. Church Street in Smithfield. During his time in Smithfield, he met his future wife, Melinda Gail Gwaltney and they were married in 2006 on Coquina Beach at the Outer Banks of North Carolina.

Apart from his interest in history and antiques, Chris has been involved in the funeral profession since 2004. At the time of this writing, he maintains an active Funeral Service License in Virginia and North Carolina. His resume includes management, funeral directing, embalming, and crematory operation duties.

www.ingramcontent.com/pod-product-compliance
Lightning Source LLC
Chambersburg PA
CBHW070043100426
42740CB00013B/2778